MW01142142

What To Do When Someone Dies:
A Legal, Financial, and Practical Guide

by

Milton Berry Scott

2nd Edition

Père Bruin Press
Alamo, California

Printed in the United States of America

Library of Congress Catalog Card Number: 97-74487

Scott, Milton Berry

What To Do When Someone Dies: A Legal, Financial, and Practical Guide—by Milton Berry Scott

ISBN: 0-9659483-4-X

Published by:

Père Bruin Press, P. O. Box 781, Alamo, California, 94507

http://www.perebruin.com

PREFACE

Many people consider the death of a loved one to be the worst experience they have to face in life. Whether the death is of a husband, wife, child, parent, brother, sister, other family member, or close friend, it is almost always a heartbreaking experience. For most of us, such times are an emotional mixture of shock and pain and uncertainty about what life will be like without that person. We are not generally at our best during such times, nor are we in an ideal state to make immediate decisions related to death and funeral arrangements, or more long term financial and legal decisions, some of which may be critical. Yet these are the things which we are faced with when someone dies. Sometimes we face these decisions alone, and sometimes we face them with other family members. This can bring its own set of complications. It's a painful reality that families don't always agree on important issues. Yet, particularly in the death of a parent, family members often have to make many of these important decisions together.

This book is a guidebook to lead you through some of the decisions and considerations that you are likely to face when someone dies. These can be broken down into the following four broad categories.

IMMEDIATE PRACTICAL CONCERNS

There are immediate practical concerns related to the death itself, burial or cremation of the body, and finding the original copy of the will (if there is a will). All of these need to dealt with within a few days of the death. While often the most emotionally overwhelming of the concerns dealt with in this book, these are usually relatively easy to deal with. However, disagreements can arise when it is unclear what the decedent wanted or if friends and relatives have strong opposing opinions.

- When Someone is Dying
- Anatomical Gifts
- Autopsy
- Choosing a Funeral Home, Mortuary, or Cremation Society

- Funeral Arrangements
- Burial or Cremation Arrangements
- Death Certificate
- Obituary
- Finding the Will

LEGAL CONCERNS

Then there are the legal concerns. The level of complexity involved here depends on how well the decedent planned his or her estate and on the value of the estate. Many times the survivors are fearful of legal complications, and it turns out that the decedent's affairs have been well planned, and only a few forms and signatures are necessary to transfer assets out of the decedent's name. Then there is the other extreme, where no planning at all has been done, and it might take the lawyers and accountants years to sort things out.

- Getting an Attorney
- List of Assets
- Personal Items and Pets
- Probate
- Transferring Assets
- If the Decedent Had a Trust
- If the Decedent Was a Trustee, Executor, or Fiduciary
- Wrongful Death Action

FINANCIAL CONCERNS

There are financial concerns related to the person's salary, credit cards, social security, insurance, pension or benefits. While these often merge into the legal concerns covered in the previous section, they are generally distinct enough to merit their own discussion.

- Paying the Bills
- Continuing Business After Death
- Valuing Assets
- Casualty Insurance for Assets
- Safe Deposit Box
- Medical Insurance

- Social Security
- Retirement and Annuity Benefits
- Credit Cards, Unpaid Salary, and Uncashed Travelers Checks
- Lump Sum Pension, Profit Sharing, IRA, and other Benefits
- Workman's Compensation Benefits
- Life Insurance

TAX CONCERNS

Finally, there are tax concerns. While they are discussed last in this book, these are the issues that might cost the survivors the most money. Even if the decedent has planned ahead, there will probably be tax returns to be filed and at least some tax due. If the decedent hasn't planned carefully, (or even in some cases when he or she has), there might be substantial taxes due.

- Final Income Tax Returns
- Gift Tax Returns
- Federal Estate Tax Return
- United States Federal Estate Tax Rates
- Generation-skipping Transfer Tax Returns
- State Inheritance and Estate Tax Returns
- Fiduciary Tax Returns

While real life is never as neat as the divisions in a book, you should anticipate having to face the immediate practical concerns in the days immediately following someone's death, the legal and financial concerns from about a week to several months after someone's death (and sometimes longer), and the tax concerns for a year or two after someone's death. Of course this schedule is a generalization, but it is a perhaps useful rough guide.

USING THIS BOOK

While this book is a guidebook, it is not a do-it-yourself guidebook. There are legal self-help books that will show you how to do everything from writing your own will to filing a lawsuit. The book you are holding in your hands merely tells you what needs to be done when someone dies. It does not tell you to do it by yourself. Unless the *decedent* (the person who died) was very poor, you are probably going to need some professional help with the legal, financial, and tax concerns.

Why (you might ask) do I need this book if I'm going to have my attorney, accountant, financial planner, or other professional help me with many of these concerns? If you have an attorney, accountant, or other planner whom you trust completely and whom you can count on to be readily available to help you with all of these concerns when someone dies, then perhaps you don't need this book. More likely though, you have an attorney who will help you with some of these concerns, an accountant who will help you with others, and perhaps some sort of financial planner who will help you with still others. This book can give you the larger picture about all of these concerns. It can also help prepare you so that you know what information to have ready for the attorney, accountant, or planner. If they are billing you at an hourly rate, this can save you money.

Many people have strong feelings regarding having to pay fees to an attorney, accountant, or other professional after someone's death. Sometimes such concerns are justified. There are dishonest and unethical attorneys, financial planners and others. However, when you are dealing with legal, financial, and tax concerns, it is important to get sound, competent advice. While it is possible to deal with many of these concerns yourself, most people do not have the time, knowledge, or inclination to deal with all of these concerns on their own. In most situations, you will save money in the long run by getting good professional advice now.

PLAN AHEAD

It's easy to second-guess decisions that you or someone else has already made. Planning ahead is always a bit trickier. When using this book, you might find yourself wishing that the decedent had planned ahead a bit more carefully. While you can't change the decisions that someone else has made, you can plan ahead for your own death and make things easier for your loved ones. The relevant sections in this book contain a *Plan Ahead* section which outlines what you can do now to make life easier for your loved ones when you die. A little bit of work on your part now can save someone else a whole lot of work and stress when you die.

Planning ahead is extremely important. However this book has been written to cover the average scenario: the decedent has done little or no planning, and it is up to you, the nearest relatives or friends, to work through the myriad of decisions which must be made. This book is a guide to the general considerations that you are likely to face, not a comprehensive encyclopedia with specific instructions to cover every conceivable situation. Furthermore, since laws and legal terms vary from state to state, it is not possible to go into a great amount of specific detail on all issues. As the plan-ahead paragraphs indicate, planning ahead is not entirely a do-it-yourself project. While many people would be happiest doing everything entirely by themselves, planning ahead means discussing some issues with loved ones and others with professionals. The situations where everyone agrees on what needs to be done are always the easiest for the survivors.

UPDATES

Nothing changes faster than tax matters. While the content of this book is up-to-date as of this writing, changes do occur, and it is the intention of the publisher that any changes affecting the content of this book will be covered in a continuous and ongoing update of this book at the Père Bruin web site: www.perebruin.com.

CONTENTS

IMMEDIATE PRACTICAL CONCERNS

When someone dies, you can generally find an attorney to help you with the legal concerns and an accountant or financial planner to help you with the financial and tax concerns. But for at least some of the immediate, practical concerns, you are on your own.

There are often medical and financial decisions to be made while someone is dying. Are there documents allowing someone else to make medical or financial decisions when the dying person is too sick to make or articulate such decisions himself or herself? *Yes: ma*

Most of us live to a relatively old age. But in cases where someone dies young, particularly in traffic accidents, some of the decedent's body might be needed as an anatomical gift. Just as the loved ones are reeling with the news of an unexpected death, they are hit with the delicate question of using the decedent's body organs. Most of us will die in a hospital, attended by a physician. But again, this isn't always the case. If there is any question as to the causes or circumstances of a death, there might be an autopsy or coroner's inquest. However, these cases are the exception rather than the rule.

For every death, decisions have to made regarding a funeral home, mortuary, or cremation society. This is true even in cases where the decedent didn't want any sort of service. Rarely has the decedent left instructions as to what should be done. Decisions need to be made regarding burial or cremation. Some of these decisions might need to be made within a few hours of the death. Once you have chosen a funeral home or mortuary, someone there will generally issue the death certificate, write an obituary, and help you through any other steps which need to be taken. If there is going to be a memorial service, this needs to be planned. Where and when will the service be held and what sort of service will it be?

Many people begin worrying about the legal and financial concerns and are on the phone to an attorney or accountant within a few hours of the death. There is usually no need for such a rush. While there are exceptions, such as cases where the decedent has been involved in an important business deal that is ready to close or has signed a contract to sell real estate but not completed the transaction, in most cases the legal and financial concerns can wait a few weeks. With most deaths, it is probably wiser for the survivors to give themselves time to deal with some of the emotional issues related to the death before moving on to deal with the financial, legal, and tax concerns. However, one issue which should be dealt within a few days, is locating the original will.

What to do with a will, or what to do if there isn't a will, is dealt with in the section on legal concerns. However, many of the decisions which you will ultimately have to make and which are discussed in later sections of this book depend on whether or not there is a will and what the will might contain.

This section should prove useful as a guide for most of the issues which you will have to face in the first week or so after the death. Obviously, this isn't an exhaustive list of every possible scenario which everyone might ever face, but it covers the basics. Dealing with grief is beyond the scope of this book, but you might take some comfort from the fact that most people face these concerns at some point and that however complicated the legal, financial, or tax concerns might be, you will probably find them much easier to deal with than the immediate concerns described here.

WHEN SOMEONE IS DYING

Some people die peacefully in their sleep, while others die suddenly of heart failure or in traffic accidents. As medical technology progresses and grows more advanced, more and more people die in hospitals, often after protracted illnesses. It is not ideal to start estate planning when someone is dying. Depending on the person's condition, there are some things you cannot do. A will dictated by a relative and signed in the hospital room where the person dies a short time later is a will that quite possibly may be challenged by a disinherited relative who does not like it. Nor is the dying person's state of mind the only one that might be open to question. Family dramas between siblings who don't get along, children and step-parents, and others frequently erupt when someone is dying in the hospital. Unresolved family problems often arise at just the time when hard and difficult decisions need to be made.

What should you do if you find yourself in such a situation? One place to start is to find out whom, if anyone, the dying person has authorized to make his or her decisions. In most states, this is done by way of a document called a power of attorney. While laws and terms vary from state to state, these documents generally come in two types, a form for health care decisions and a document for general financial affairs.

Most states have a standardized form by which someone can indicate a number of things they want regarding health care decisions. The form indicates who a person wants to make his or her health care decisions should he or she become incapacitated (unable to make coherent decisions.) If the person has completed such a form, find it. The person named to make decisions should be in contact with the doctors and should make any necessary decisions. The hospital, health care organization, and doctor will also probably want copies of the document to keep on file.

The other type of power of attorney covers financial decisions. This becomes important in situations where someone is incapacitated some time before death. Who has the right to handle the person's financial affairs? A general durable power of attorney, power of attorney, or durable power of attorney (as it is called in many states) is usually a two to ten page document naming someone (and often an alternate) to make financial decisions on behalf of someone should the person become incapacitated. If the person has such a document, the person named as the agent should have a copy so that he or she can present it to banks, brokerage houses, or other financial institutions when making financial transactions on the person's behalf.

Many people have living trusts. Here, the trust agreement or declaration, as it is called, usually names a successor trustee to take over the management of the trust assets if the current trustee resigns, dies, or becomes incapacitated. If John Doe has a living trust and he is the sole trustee, upon his death another trustee is named. It may be a bank trust department, his daughter, or his four children jointly. Look through the trust document and see who is named as the successor trustee. A copy of the trust should be available so the next named trustee may take over the trust immediately and handle the trust assets.

Making sure that someone's health care decisions are being properly made and that financial affairs are covered by a power of attorney and the successor trustee of a living trust, if the person has a trust, are probably the most important issues to consider when someone is ill and dying. The larger concern which often arises in such cases is that of what the person has done in terms of estate planning.

Someone's deathbed is not the place to start estate planning. If he or she is likely to die within a couple of days, it is probably too late to do much of anything. However if the person is likely to live for a few more weeks, is in good mental condition, and there is a doctor who will certify, if necessary, that the person is mentally fit and aware of his or her actions, there might be time to find an attorney to do some rudimentary estate planning.

Another situation which sometimes arises is that of a person who is mentally incapacitated, does not have a power of attorney to cover financial affairs, and yet lives for some time. If there is a spouse, he or she will frequently have access to bank and brokerage accounts and be able to handle most financial matters. But in cases where there is no spouse, it is sometimes necessary to obtain a conservatorship. This usually difficult, time-consuming affair will involve court hearings and obtaining an attorney. If you think you are facing such a situation, contact an attorney to see what options are available.

• PLAN AHEAD

This is not a book on estate planning. However, a small amount of effort on your part now will make life much easier for your survivors when you die. While some people are indifferent as to what happens to them as they lie dying in a hospital, most have strong feelings about the matter. At the time of this writing, health care service and attitudes towards dying are in a state of flux and change. Contact your doctor, health care organization, or attorney and find out about the form (durable power of attorney for health care, living will, etc.) which you can fill out to allow someone to make health care decisions for you if you become incapacitated and unable to make such decisions. Talk to an attorney about the document (called a general durable power of attorney in most states) that will allow someone to manage your financial assets should you become incapacitated. If you have a living trust, review the trust document to determine who manages the trust assets in the event of your death or incapacity.

Finally, let your loved ones know now how you feel about important medical decisions which you might face, how you want your financial affairs handled should you become too ill to handle them, and who you want to make these decisions for you should you become unable to do so yourself.

If you have several children and are naming one child to make medical decisions and handle financial affairs, be sure to tell all of the children of this arrangement. Nothing can cause greater strife in a family than for the children to learn after death that one child is in charge of everything instead of all of the children jointly. Avoid this potential problem by publicizing your wishes to all of the children before you die or become incapacitated. You do not have to ask for their approval; just tell them how you have set things up so they are aware of your decision.

ANATOMICAL GIFTS

Most of us will die at a relatively advanced age when our body organs will be past their prime. But not everyone lives to an old age. Death is always hard to face, but it is even harder in cases when the decedent should have had many years left to live. Depending on the nature of the death, parts of the decedent's body might be requested for transplant purposes. Body parts and organs, such as heart, kidneys, and liver are often desperately needed for transplants. In the case of the death of a young or even middle-aged person, this is often the first decision that you, the survivor, will have to make. Do you want to authorize an organ donation?

Even if the person has left clear, written consent for the donation of body organs, most medical organizations which handle transplants will generally not accept a donation without the written consent of the nearest relative or relatives. So, whatever the decedent's wishes, the decision ultimately rests with you. Making the decision by yourself can be hard. It is easier if there are several relatives making the decision—provided that they all agree. The most difficult decisions occur when the relatives disagree. Depending on the circumstances, if the nearest relatives don't agree on what should be done, no action can be taken and the anatomical gift can't be made. Since most of us would want our views respected on such matters, it is logical to do what the decedent wished if he or she specified his or her wishes.

The decedent might have made an authorization by a signed, written document (possibly handwritten), by his or her will, by filling out a card issued by the state Department of Motor Vehicles, or by filling out a Durable Power of Attorney for Health Care form or similar document which gives the person named as agent the authority to make such a decision. The problem with any of these is that they are rarely at hand at the hospital when the decedent dies. Hopefully, you, as the nearest surviving relative, will know what the decedent's wishes were and act accordingly. If you are not sure, you can only guess what the decedent would have wanted.

If you haven't discussed these issues with the decedent and aren't sure what he or she would have wanted, try to check the decedent's records. (You will probably be working under severe time constraints since anatomical gifts generally need to be made within a few hours of death.) Are there any written documents at home relating to anatomical gifts? Is there a clause in the will (if there is a will) relating to anatomical gifts? If this situation occurs during normal business hours, you might be able to make a quick phone call to the decedent's attorney, who might be able to check a copy of the will for such instructions.

If the decedent failed to leave any instructions, then the nearest relative or relatives have the right to make a decision regarding the donation of body organs. (While the executor named in the will might indeed be a relative, the executor usually does not have power as such to make this sort of decision.) The right to make decisions regarding anatomical gifts generally descends in the following order: 1) spouse, 2) children, 3) grandchildren, 4) parents, 5) brothers and sisters, 6) other relatives.

• PLAN AHEAD

None of us intends to die before our time. Nevertheless, some of us will. Spare your loved ones the anguish of debate over your body parts and make your desires on this subject known. Tell your nearest relatives whether you want your body parts donated or not.

Most states have a card which can be attached to the back of the driver's license which authorizes donation of needed organs or tissue upon your death. Fill out this card. You can agree to donate any needed organs or parts, or only certain specified organs or parts (which you write in), or you decline to donate anything. (This card is generally only legal for drivers 18 or over, and thus wouldn't apply to 16 or 17 year olds.) Presumably you keep your driver's license in your wallet or purse, but let your nearest relatives know if it's somewhere else.

Some attorneys recommend putting a section in the will regarding anatomical gifts, but I don't. Anatomical gifts generally need to be taken from the body within a few hours of death. A copy of the will is rarely at hand, and it might be some time before it can be found. I recommend drafting a document along the following lines:

"At my death I wish any needed body organs to be used for transplant purposes. I authorize my relatives and executor to sign any necessary documents to carry this out."

Other attorneys recommend putting this information in a Durable Power of Attorney for Health Care Decisions (or similar document). This is a legal document covering many potential health related situations in addition to the donation of body organs. The problem with any written authorization is that the question of organ donations often arises in the case of sudden, unexpected deaths. Decisions have to be made at very short notice, and these written authorizations usually cannot be found and produced in the necessary time span. Hence, you should really let your loved ones know what your wishes are on this matter.

AUTOPSY

When someone dies from natural causes and has been seen by a physician within a short time, such as 30 days of death, most states do not require an autopsy. However if the decedent dies in an accident, or dies by violence, or has not been attended by a physician within a specified number of days (such as 30) before death, the local county coroner's office will generally perform an autopsy. In some cases a doctor might refuse to sign a death certificate because of possible medical error and an autopsy will be required. An autopsy is a medical procedure whereby a doctor examines the body to determine the cause of death. The doctor might take blood or tissue samples from the body for further testing. The actual autopsy might typically take only a few hours. However lab work to test blood or tissue samples might take several weeks to complete. So though the autopsy is generally performed within a few days of death, it might take the coroner's office many weeks to issue the autopsy report.

After the blood and tissue samples are taken, the body is "released" by the coroner's office to the nearest relatives. The funeral home or mortuary which the relatives have chosen will, upon receiving authorization, arrange for the transfer of the body to their facility. If there is a delay due to lack of staff at the coroner's office or unusual circumstances (such as an airline crash and multiple deaths), it might be several days or even weeks before the body is released. Fortunately, such situations rarely occur.

The county pays for an autopsy required by state law. You, as the nearest surviving relative don't have to pay, although you will have to pay to get a copy of the autopsy report. That cost might vary from $25 to $100. The report typically runs from four to twenty pages. An autopsy report is not a private document. In cases where there is public interest in a death, the media can pay for and receive a copy of the autopsy report as well.

Even if the decedent does die of natural causes and has been seen by a physician within the specified number of days prior to the date of death, an autopsy can be requested by immediate family members, by an agent under a durable power of attorney for health care form or similar document, or can be directed by the decedent's will. However, if an autopsy is not required by law, the person or people who request it will have to pay the costs, which may exceed $1,000.

You would probably only want to consider requesting an autopsy if the decedent dies in an accident, if there is a suspicion of violence as the cause of death, or if you suspect that the decedent has died due to medical malpractice.

Occasionally the county coroner's office will hold a hearing, called a "coroner's inquest" to determine the cause of death. The coroner can require testimony and hear evidence to determine the legal cause of death. After the inquest is held, a death certificate is issued. A coroner's inquest is a more general inquiry about and investigation of the death than the autopsy which is merely a medical examination of the body. A coroner's inquest is very rarely held. It might be held in cases where the decedent dies in mysterious circumstances, in cases where violence is suspected, or in cases where the decedent dies alone and the body is not discovered for some time.

The coroner's office has the right to take temporary possession of the decedent's personal items such as clothing, wallet, jewelry and other items if the decedent is found dead without any relatives present. These are delivered to the executor or other relatives later. In cases where it is unclear how to reach the nearest relatives or where the will is (if there is one), a representative of the coroner's office or public administrator's office may search the decedent's residence to attempt to find the will and to find information regarding the nearest relatives to notify of the death.

CHOOSING A FUNERAL HOME, MORTUARY, OR CREMATION SOCIETY

The first decision that most people have to make when a loved one dies is choosing a funeral home or mortuary. You might think that hospitals, where people die every day, would have some special service to help relatives choose a funeral home or mortuary. However, most hospitals do not. You will most likely have to choose the funeral home or mortuary yourself. If the decedent has already made some sort of funeral, burial, or cremation arrangements, then you should follow these. If not, then you should look through the yellow pages in your local telephone directory and choose a funeral home or mortuary. The terms "funeral home" and "mortuary"' refer to the same sort of institution. A funeral home (or mortuary) will send someone to come and take the body from the hospital to the funeral home. The funeral home usually will handle the death certificate and obituary. If the body is to be cremated, it will ordinarily be done there at the funeral home, although it can be handled by a separate cremation society. If the body is to be buried, the body will be embalmed there at the funeral home. The funeral home will coordinate any funeral or memorial service with the church, synagogue, fraternal order, or veterans group where the service is held. The funeral home will arrange the actual burial or cremation. Normally the funeral home or mortuary will notify the social security administration to discontinue future payments if the decedent was receiving social security. If the decedent was a veteran, the funeral home will usually advise the relatives regarding whether a death benefit is payable and may even complete the paperwork.

The staff at most funeral homes are skilled at dealing with the emotional and practical problems which arise when someone dies. Should there be a service at the funeral home or at church? Should the casket be present or not? If the casket is at the service, should it be open or not? One guide to answering these questions is knowing what the decedent wanted. Did the decedent leave any written instructions regarding a funeral?

If the decedent died far from home and the body needs to be transported to another area, the funeral home will usually handle all of the arrangements to transport the body to a funeral home or mortuary at the other end. However, air costs can be considerable since most airlines charge first class air rates to transport a body.

The prices that funeral homes charge vary widely and depend on whether there is a funeral, burial, or cremation service. Another factor is geography. If you live in a major city, the funeral home will generally cost a lot more than in a small town.

One alternative to a funeral home or mortuary is a cremation society. These are usually less expensive than a funeral home since the body is cremated immediately after it is taken from the hospital. If you know that the decedent wanted to be cremated, this is one option which you might want to consider.

It is possible that the decedent completed paperwork with a funeral home or cremation society before his or her death. This is sometimes referred to as a "pre-need" arrangement. In this case, the decedent has already completed most of the arrangements for the funeral and burial or cremation. Pre-need arrangements generally involve paying most costs at the time the arrangement is made. This can include the purchase of a plot in a cemetery. Although many funeral homes demand payment at the time the pre-need arrangement is made, some will take a down payment and allow the balance to be paid at the time of the decedent's death. Costs not included in a pre-need agreement might include the costs of obtaining a death certificate, opening and closing the grave, and preparing the headstone.

Find out if the decedent had a pre-need agreement before you choose a funeral home or mortuary. If you choose a funeral home or mortuary and then later discover that the decedent had a pre-need agreement with a different one, you probably won't be able to get any sort of a refund.

- ## PLAN AHEAD

If you have any reason to believe that you are going to die in the near future, make a pre-need arrangement with a local funeral home, mortuary, or cremation society. Even if you intend to live for many years, you might have strong feelings about the matter and want to make such an arrangement now. If you do, make sure that your loved ones are aware of it. Even if you don't make a pre-need arrangement, let your loved ones know whether you would prefer a burial or cremation.

FUNERAL ARRANGEMENTS

Once you have arranged for the body to be taken to a funeral home or mortuary the next consideration is the funeral service. What sort of funeral or memorial service did the decedent want?

If the decedent was a member of a church or synagogue, it might be appropriate to have a funeral service there. Hopefully, the decedent made his or her wishes known. If not, the decision falls to you. Most churches will help arrange such a service even if the decedent wasn't an active member of the church. However the costs or donation involved might be higher for someone who wasn't a member of the church.

If the decedent was a member of a Masonic or other fraternal organization, a special memorial service by the order can often be arranged. Funeral homes and mortuaries often help arrange such services. Contact the order if this seems appropriate. If the decedent was a veteran and you want to arrange a military funeral, contact the local veteran's administration for information. The funeral home or mortuary can advise you whether this is possible and what procedural and legal requirements are involved.

If the decedent hasn't left specific instructions, you should spend time planning the service. Some of the things to consider include what musical selections should be played, whether the music should be played by an organist, other soloist, larger group, or even if taped pre-recorded music should be played. Should there be a reading from the Bible or other religious work? Should there be a reading of poetry or perhaps some other literary selection? Who will do the reading? Most services have a eulogy in which someone, whether a minister or family member, speaks about the life of the deceased. Often a number of people speak. If a minister who was not well acquainted with the deceased is giving the eulogy, you will probably want to spend time giving him or her the necessary biographical material. Most ministers, rabbis, and other religious personnel are used to spending time discussing the deceased with family members and then giving a tasteful eulogy of perhaps ten to fifteen minutes at the service. There are, of course, no rules as to how long a service should last, but services typically run 35-45 minutes. There is also generally a short reception with food afterwards so that friends and relatives can meet with the family.

In some cases a memorial service might be held weeks or even a month or more after the decedent's death. Sometimes such a delay allows busy friends and relatives the time necessary to arrange their schedules to attend. But most services are held within a week of the death. And, if the decedent was Jewish and the body is not embalmed, services might be held within 48 hours of death.

• **PLAN AHEAD**

Some people don't care what sort of funeral will be held for them after they die. Others want to plan the whole thing, including special messages to be read and the hymns to be sung. Whether you incline toward either of these extremes or fall somewhere in between, it will probably help your loved ones if you at least choose whether or not you want a service (many people don't), whether it is to be a church service or not, whether the casket is to be at the service, and where you would like the service to be held. Writing down your wishes now can also save problems later on, especially if different family members attend different churches or for whatever other reasons might have conflicting ideas about the way a service should be held.

BURIAL OR CREMATION ARRANGEMENTS

Once you have arranged to have the body taken to a funeral home. mortuary, or cremation society, decisions need to be made regarding the burial or cremation. Again, if the decedent has left written instructions, these should be carried out. If there are no written instructions but the decedent has signed a Durable Power of Attorney for Health Care or similar form, the agent can make the decisions. If there are no written instructions and no Durable Power of Attorney for Health Care or similar form and agent, then the decisions fall to you, the decedent's nearest relatives.

Did the decedent want to be buried or cremated? Some religions don't allow cremation, so this won't be an option for everyone. If the decedent wanted to be buried, had he or she bought a burial plot? In some cases where a family has lived in the same area for many generations, there might even be a family plot. If the decedent has made some sort of arrangements, you will need to find a document called the cemetery deed. The funeral home or mortuary will want this deed before proceeding with burial arrangements. If the decedent wanted to be buried but had not made some prior arrangements, what plots are available? A representative of the funeral home should be able to help you with this.

If the decedent wished to be cremated, you need to decide what to do with the ashes. Ashes cannot be scattered on private property in many states, even with the permission of the owner. Other states allow such scattering if you have written permission. Ashes can be placed in a mausoleum or a common area of a cemetery which holds ashes. Ashes can also be scattered at sea; sometimes ashes can be scattered on land, but the rules on this vary greatly from state to state. It might cost $500 to $1,000 to place ashes in a mausoleum. Some of the less expensive cremation societies might charge $400 to $500 for a cremation and perhaps another $100 for scattering the ashes at sea.

If the deceased was a member of a fraternal order, a special burial service by the order can frequently be arranged. If a veteran, then the veteran's administration needs to be contacted to determine if burial at a veteran's cemetery is available.

- **PLAN AHEAD**

People are often more particular about what happens to their bodies after their deaths than they are about their funeral services. Make your wishes known to your loved ones regarding your preferences for burial or cremation and where you want to be buried or where you want the ashes placed or scattered. If you want to be buried and you live in a densely populated area, perhaps you should look into a burial plot now. If you do buy a burial plot before your death, make sure that your loved ones know where the cemetery deed is located so that they can find it easily after your death. If you are a veteran and want a veteran's service, let your loved ones know where your discharge papers and any other relevant documents are.

DEATH CERTIFICATE

Normally an employee of the funeral home or cremation society will prepare the death certificate. Once the form has been prepared, the employee will get the signature of the physician attending the decedent at the time of death or that of the coroner and then file the original copy of the death certificate with the county or local health department of the county in which the decedent died.

The person preparing the death certificate will probably ask for some of the following information from the family or relatives to complete the form. (Forms vary from state to state.)

- date of the decedent's birth
- place of the decedent's birth
- decedent's social security number
- date and time of decedent's death
- decedent's employer and occupation
- decedent's address
- name and address of the informant (the person supplying this information)
- names and birthplaces of both of the decedent's parents
- name of the decedent's surviving spouse
- maiden name of the decedent's mother
- date and place of the disposition (the funeral home or mortuary to which the body is taken)
- place of death

The person preparing the death certificate will also get information from the attending physician regarding the cause of death and then get the physician's certification. The death certificate is then filed at the county health department or with the county recorder.

If any of information listed above is later found to be incorrect, an amended form can be prepared and filed at that time.

You will need certified copies of the death certificate to deal with some of the legal and financial concerns discussed in later sections of this book. These certified copies will be needed for termination of joint tenancy, for life insurance policies, for IRA accounts and pension plans, and for dealing with other assets. The number of certified copies which you need might run from two or three copies all the way up to 80-100 copies.

Very few organizations will accept photocopies of the death certificate. Most require a certified copy bearing the official seal of the county or issuing government organization.

In those rare cases where the decedent was not treated by a physician within a certain number of days of death or where the person died by violent means, accident or under mysterious circumstances, an autopsy may be required. If the cause of death is not known, a temporary death certificate can be issued by the county coroner's office. A permanent death certificate is then issued later.

Generally, the person from the funeral home or mortuary handling the death certificate will file it within three to four days, although in very unusual circumstances this can be as long as six to eight weeks.

The cost of a certified copy of the death certificate varies from state to state and county to county, but is generally somewhere around $5-15 per copy. Usually the funeral home or mortuary will order five to ten copies for you. You can order more later, if you need to, either through the funeral home or directly from the county department.

If the decedent died in a state other than the one in which he or she lived, the local health department or agency in that state will issue the death certificate. If the decedent died overseas and was a United States citizen, the State Department will issue a form entitled "Report of the Death of an American Citizen Abroad." This form (federal form OF-180) can be obtained for a fee from the State Department. It is treated as a formal death certificate. To get such a form contact the U.S. Department of State, Washington D.C. 20524.

OBITUARY NOTICE

The obituary notice is generally handled by the funeral home or mortuary. Most newspapers have a fixed format, so that the names of relatives, organizations and other information may be inserted. You can generally deviate from this format if you want to add additional information or leave out standard information. However, newspaper space considerations limit the number of words an obituary can run. Most newspapers now charge from $75-$250 to run an obituary.

While formats vary from newspaper to newspaper, the following items are typically included.

- name
- city of residence
- year of birth
- most recent occupation and years employed
- significant prior jobs
- education
- clubs and civic activities
- military service
- any publications
- any significant awards or citations
- anything else of unusual interest
- names of surviving spouse and mention of children and any grandchildren or great-grandchildren (sometimes names will be mentioned, space permitting)
- family preferences regarding donations to charities (Families generally specify if they would prefer money donated to a charity in lieu of a gift of flowers to the family.)

Many obituaries list the time of the funeral or memorial service. It has been common for robbers to read such notices, know that they'll be likely to find an empty house while everyone is at the service, and proceed to plunder the house during the service. One way to prevent this is to have someone stay at the decedent's house during the service and guard the house.

• PLAN AHEAD

If you have strong feelings about how you want your obituary to read, you can write it out now. If the thought of writing your obituary in advance sounds macabre, remember that news organizations generally have obituaries on file for most celebrities and major public figures. If the celebrity should die suddenly and unexpectedly, the obituary can be published immediately. While there is no particular practical value to writing your obituary before you die, it might give you some satisfaction to emphasize the aspects of your life which you want remembered.

FINDING THE WILL

If the decedent had a will, you need to find the original copy. This is either the will which has been signed by the decedent and witnesses or a holographic will entirely in the decedent's handwriting. (Laws vary from state to state regarding what constitutes a legally admissible will.) Many of the decisions which you must make and which will be discussed in later sections of this book depend on whether there is a will, and if there is, what is in the will.

The original will must be deposited with the county in which the decedent resided within a limited time after the date of death. (This period varies from state to state, but it might typically be around 30 days.) In those rare instances where someone dies but no one learns of it until later, the original will must be deposited with the county within a specified period based on when a custodian of the will learned of the death. (Again, the specified time varies from state to state.) There generally is no charge for depositing a will with the county. All original wills, whether witnessed or handwritten, should be deposited. Depositing the will usually consists of mailing the original and a copy to the county courthouse. There someone stamps the original to indicate that it has been officially deposited, stamps the copy, and then mails the copy back to you, keeping the original. There is generally no fee for this. Copies of the will might also have to be mailed to other parties such as the executor named in the will.

If there is going to be a probate proceeding, the original will must be deposited with the court in order to start the probate proceeding.

The original will may be held by the attorney who drafted it. Many attorneys and legal firms retain the original will for their clients. Unfortunately, sometimes the client may move away, lose his or her copy of the will, or forget what happened to the original copy.

Many people put the original will in their safe deposit box. In some states, the safe deposit box is sealed at death and cannot be entered until a representative of the state tax department inventories the contents of the box. An appointment may be necessary to have the box inventoried and this might take several weeks.

In many states the safe deposit box is not sealed or inventoried at death. If there is a co-signer on the box, the co-signer may legally enter the box and remove any contents, including the will. But even if you are not a co-signer, if you have the key to the box and a certified copy of the death certificate, you can generally enter the box to look for the original will. In such cases, a representative of the bank or savings and loan will accompany you to make sure that you take nothing else from the box. If you can't find the key, you can usually have someone from the bank or savings and loan drill the box open. This might cost around $100.

Many times, the original will is retained by the individual at home.

If the original will cannot be found and the decedent had custody of the will before death, there may be the presumption that the will was voluntarily destroyed. In many cases, copies of the will are not valid.

• PLAN AHEAD

Since this is not a book on estate planning or wills, there isn't space here to discuss the issue of why you should have a will. Unless you are very, very poor, you probably need a will and moreover, one that is up to date. Let your immediate relatives or friends know where the original copy of the will is so that they can find it easily after your death. You may wish to give a photocopy of the will to the executor and the people who inherit your estate. It also is generally a good idea to have someone as a co-signer on your safe deposit box. This allows the person to enter the safe deposit box after your death, whether the box is inventoried or not.

LEGAL
CONCERNS

The immediate, practical concerns that you have to deal with after someone dies are generally the most upsetting since they must be dealt with right after the person dies. Once the funeral and burial or cremation have taken place, most people just want to be left alone with their grief and not have to deal with more details and decisions.

Unfortunately, the immediate concerns are just the beginning of an ongoing legal, financial, and tax process that might take a year or more to complete. While there is some overlap among these concerns (certain financial concerns affect tax and other matters), it is probably best to discuss these issues one at a time. For that reason I have grouped these matters into the three large categories of legal, financial, and tax concerns.

Most people are probably vaguely aware that when a person dies the decedent's property passes to someone. Most people know at least something about wills. Many people have heard of probate and know that it is a lengthy and costly legal procedure. However, there are other legal concerns of which you should be aware. Many of these have time limits. Laws and time limits vary from state to state, but they typically concern actions which must be taken or documents which must be filed within so many days or months of the decedent's death.

Many people are hesitant to contact attorneys since they feel that most attorneys are dishonest and will charge them exorbitant bills. While many concerns regarding attorneys and their billing practices are justified, it will generally save you money in the long run to get competent legal advice when someone dies rather than try to do it all yourself and later find out that you have done something wrong and created problems and complications.

One way to keep the attorney's bill down is to have as much of the necessary information beforehand as possible. This section discusses the sort of information you will need regarding the decedent's assets which you can bring to the attorney. With that information in hand, you and the attorney can then discuss the best way to transfer the decedent's assets to whoever inherits it with the least amount of time and cost. If the decedent has planned his or her estate carefully, this might involve no more than signing a few documents. If, on the other hand, the decedent's financial affairs are complicated and if the decedent hasn't planned his or her estate well, the legal issues might take many months or even years to sort out.

Another point is that what people think are the important legal issues and what the important legal issues actually are often are two very different things. Families and others do, of course, sometimes fight over the decedent's assets. A far more common occurrence though, is for family members to fight bitterly over personal items which have little if any financial value but which have emotional connotations. You need to be able to differentiate between the genuine legal issues involved and family disagreements, and make an effort to keep the latter from escalating into legal conflict. I have personally seen more time and money wasted on family disagreements than on anything else in the many years I have been practicing law.

This section should give you a rough idea of what general legal issues you need to consider and the information which an attorney or other professional will need to help you. Again, laws and regulations vary from state to state, so this is not a definitive checklist. Nevertheless, it will give you an idea of most of the issues involved for most situations.

GETTING AN ATTORNEY

If the decedent was very poor, it's quite possible that you don't need an attorney. On the other hand, the decedent might have been quite wealthy with complicated financial affairs. But if he or she planned very carefully for death, you might only need an attorney to check over a few documents at a small cost. However, these are the extremes. In most cases you will need an attorney to deal with these legal concerns.

You should probably contact an attorney within a few days of the ✓ decedent's death. Just as important as finding an attorney is finding one that you trust. Another important issue is finding an attorney who is knowledgeable about estate planning. "Estate planning" is the general term for the area of law involving death-related legal issues. ✓

If the decedent had an attorney who had drafted his or her will and ✓ helped with other estate planning issues, you should contact him or her. This attorney should be familiar with the specific details and circumstances of the decedent's estate and what legal concerns are relevant. However, if for some reason you find that you are not comfortable with the decedent's attorney or you don't entirely trust him or her, you can always go to another attorney. An attorney does not own a client's files. In most states, an attorney is obligated by law to hand over any relevant files.

While you can look for an attorney in the yellow pages it is probably better to ask around and find one recommended by someone you know. You can ask your accountant, financial planner, or any other financial professional you know. If asked, banks and savings and loans will often recommend an estate planning attorney. If you have an attorney, but one who specializes in an area other than estate planning, he or she probably knows an estate planning specialist whom he or she can recommend.

An estate planning attorney will advise you regarding the legal concerns listed here as well as regarding many of the financial and tax concerns. The legal concern which many people worry about the most after someone's death is the question of whether there is going to be a probate or not. Generally speaking, assets in the decedent's name alone go through probate. Probate is necessary when the decedent had more than a certain amount of assets in his or her name alone and does not have a surviving spouse or does not leave the assets to the surviving spouse. The amount that the decedent can have in his or her name alone varies from state to state. The attorney can advise you on the limit. Assets held in joint tenancy, assets with a named beneficiary, and assets in a living trust do not go through probate.

An attorney will help you sort out how these different types of assets must be handled. If a probate is necessary, the attorney will guide you through it. If you are named as the executor or executrix of the will, the attorney will guide you through that as well.

What should you expect from an attorney? You should expect a clear explanation of who will inherit the decedent's assets and whether probate is required or not. In order to discuss these matters with an attorney you should have a general idea of the decedent's assets, their approximate value, and how title is held. Can you expect a free meeting with an attorney before committing yourself? That depends on the attorney. Some will meet prospective clients for an hour or so and then let the client decide whether or not to continue at billable hourly rates. However, many attorneys feel that their time is the prime commodity that they are selling and so charge for first meetings with clients. You shouldn't necessarily be put off by an attorney who charges for a first meeting; most experienced attorneys do. But regardless of whether the attorney charges for a first meeting or not, you should expect the attorney to be absolutely clear regarding what his or her fees and costs will be.

One final issue to consider is the question of who should see the attorney. In many cases just the husband or wife of the deceased will want to deal with the legal issues. Sometimes the children get involved; sometimes they don't. Sometimes the estate goes to the decedent's domestic partner. Generally speaking, the attorney will only represent one person, such as the decedent's spouse. If children or step-children are involved, there is generally no problem as long as everyone agrees on the basic issues. Problems arise when family members (or friends, domestic partners, or others) are in conflict. One attorney cannot represent two or more persons who are in disagreement. In such cases the conflicting persons will have to get different attorneys who will then try to work out the disagreements. This obviously increases the time (and thus the costs) of everyone involved. It's cheaper and easier for everyone to work out such disagreements without attorneys, if possible.

- ## PLAN AHEAD
If you have used an attorney to plan your estate, make sure that your family knows who the attorney is, so that they can contact him or her at the time of your death. Make sure that your family knows where your will and information regarding your assets are, so that they can have this information in hand when they meet with an attorney.

LISTING ASSETS

One of the first things which you must do is to determine what the decedent owned at the time of his or her death. Most people do not maintain any sort of list of their assets. It will probably be up to you to try to find what the person owned.

You will need to get or make up a list of all assets which the decedent owned, such as real estate, securities, bank and savings and loan accounts, brokerage accounts, mutual funds, life insurance, IRA, and any other assets worth more than a few hundred dollars. It does not matter if these assets are in a living trust, joint tenancy with another person, or have a designated beneficiary. All assets owned by the decedent, regardless of title or beneficiary, should be listed. These will be needed in valuing assets and for tax considerations. If no other information is available, you can review the decedent's last income tax return. Schedule B of the tax return will list interest and dividends from brokerage accounts, stocks and bonds, and bank accounts.

Here is a list of the sorts of things you should know or have regarding the decedent's assets:

1. Real Property
- Address
- Date Purchased
- Cost Basis
- Title to Property
- Current Value
- Amount of Mortgage and Lender
- Assessor or County's number for property
- Copy of the Deed
- Copy of the Mortgage
- Last Real Estate Tax Bill

You should have each of these for each parcel of real property.

2. Bank, Savings and Loan, Credit Union and Thrift Accounts
- Name of Institution
- Branch Address
- Type of Account
- Current Balance
- Title to Account
- Passbook Certificate or Statement

You should have each of these for each account.

3. Stock Certificates
- Name of Security and Number of Shares
- Date Purchased
- Cost Basis
- Title
- Current Value
- Type of Preferred Stock (if the stock is preferred)

4. Bonds
- Bonds or Statement Showing Bonds
- Face Amount of Bond
- Name of Bond
- Type of Bond
- Interest Rate
- Due Date
- Date Purchased
- Cost Basis
- Title
- Current Value

5. Mutual Funds
- Statement for each Fund
- Exact Name of Fund (Some funds have 60-80 sub funds.)
- Number of Shares
- Date Purchased
- Cost Basis

- Title
- Current Value

6. Limited Partnership
- Last K-1 Tax Form for Partnership
- Name of Partnership
- Address of General Partner
- Date Purchased
- Cost Basis
- Title
- Current Value

7. Brokerage Accounts
- Brokerage Statement (for each account)
- Name and Location
- Account Number
- Title
- Current Value

8. Notes and Mortgages Due You
- Payor on Note
- Exact Name of Payee
- Due Date
- Interest Rate
- Balance
- Title
- Security (if any) for Note

9. Other Assets (Relevant information for other substantial assets such as automobile, boat, airplane, antiques, copyrights, oil or gas royalties, or business interest.)

How do you value these assets? The Internal Revenue Service provides that for stocks and bonds you obtain the average between the high and low for the date of death. If the person died on the weekend, you can take the average between the high and low for Friday and the high and low for Monday.

For mutual funds, you take the bid price of the fund on the last trading day after the date of death.

For notes, and bank and savings and loan accounts, use the balance as of the date of death.

For limited partnerships, the general partner should be able to provide information on valuation.

Real estate values for a home and other properties can be obtained by a local real estate broker or agent. For some real estate, it may be necessary to get an appraisal by a qualified appraiser.

For other assets, the value is what you could sell the asset for as of the date of death.

• **PLAN AHEAD**

You can save your loved ones a lot of time and stress after your death by compiling a list now of the assets that you own. A list such as this is only useful if it is up to date. It doesn't do anyone much good if you make up such a list and then leave it in a drawer for ten years. When someone then reviews it after your death, it will almost surely be out of date. People's financial situations change over time. Every time that yours changes, update the list.

PERSONAL ITEMS and PETS

While most people would expect disagreements involving large sums of money, the fact is that survivors more often fight over the personal items of the decedent. Similarly, when planning their estates, people often put more effort into deciding who will receive this or that personal item or how a pet will be cared for after the owner's death than with the larger financial dispositions.

Pets obviously need to be fed and cared for, so a decision about the pet or pets has to be made within a very short time of the decedent's death. In many cases, especially where the decedent has been ill beforehand, arrangements will have been made. In some cases, people specify in their wills or other documents who they want to care for a beloved pet. Sometimes though, it won't be clear what to do with the pet. In such situations, you will have to balance what the decedent would have wanted with practical considerations. If at all possible, a pet should go to someone who will love and care for it. If you can't find someone, contact a local animal shelter, humane society, or similar organization where someone should be able to help you place the pet. In many states it is against the law to direct that at your death the pet also be put to death.

The decedent's personal items are usually covered in the decedent's will if he or she had one. Sometimes specific items are left to specific people, and sometimes all of the personal items are left to a single person such as the decedent's spouse. Often though, the personal items are left to be divided up among the several people, such as the decedent's children. In many cases, the children or others can agree on who gets what and either sell or give away any unwanted items.

Problems often arise though, especially among siblings. Perhaps one child spent more time caring for the parent than the others and feels that he or she should receive a larger share of the personal items as some sort of compensation. Sometimes brothers and sisters have disagreements going back for years that manifest themselves in a fight over some personal object. Sometimes a second spouse and a stepchild will disagree over such an object. If such disagreements arise, the best thing to do is discuss the matter openly and honestly. Sometimes having a neutral third party involved in the discussion will help in reaching an agreement.

People who persist in such disagreements should realize that such situations, if not resolved, can land up involving large amounts of time for everyone involved, including attorneys and other professionals, and hence can significantly raise legal and other fees.

• PLAN AHEAD

Plan ahead now and decide who might be able and willing to take your pet after you die. When you name someone in your will, codicil, or other document, be sure that the person involved is both willing and able to care for the pet and that you have discussed the situation thoroughly with the person beforehand.

If you intend to leave all of your personal items to one person, such as a spouse, or if you intend to have them divided among a group of people who all get along reasonably well, all you need to do is make the appropriate disposition in your will. However, if you are leaving these items to be divided among children who don't get along, a second spouse and step-children, or others who might disagree, you can deal with it in a couple of different ways.

It is possible to itemize who gets what (in as much excruciating detail as you choose) in a will or codicil. The problem with this approach is that people often change their minds as to what they want to go to whom, and hence have to pay attorney's fees to go back and modify the will or codicil. Some states allow a person to make a handwritten list or statement if it is all in the person's handwriting, dated, and signed. No witnesses are required. If your state allows this, then you can write your list by hand, tearing it up and replacing it with a new list, as needed.

The other approach is to make an disinterested outside party the executor of your will and let him or her deal with it. You can name a bank or trust company as your executor, but you should check to see if the institution is willing to serve. Most corporate fiduciaries will not handle estates below a minimum value, which may be from $300,000 to $1,000,000. There might still be disagreements, but ultimately the children or parties involved will have to abide by what the executor decides.

In any case, think about how you want to divide your personal items, and if you foresee disagreements, talk the situation over with the people involved. You can prevent some (if not all) problems later on by making sure now that everyone knows explicitly what your wishes are.

PROBATE

One concern is always whether the decedent's assets have to go through probate after the death or whether this can be avoided. Probate takes a lot of time (sometimes a year or more) and can cost a lot of money. Probate is a legal process in which a court validates the decedent's will (if there is one) and appoints someone to handle the decedent's assets and pay any taxes and outstanding bills. A simple probate might take from six to nine months. One involving an estate tax might take from 12 to 15 months. If there is litigation or other serious disagreements or problems, the probate might stretch on many months or even years longer.

ASSETS SUBJECT TO PROBATE

Probate laws vary from state to state, but generally speaking, assets in the decedent's name alone may have to go through probate. However, if these assets are left to a surviving spouse or if the value of these assets does not exceed a certain specified amount, then they are not probated. The specified amount varies from state to state. In community property states, one half of each asset registered as community property is subject to probate. The decedent's share of an asset held as tenants in common is subject to probate. Any unregistered assets such as furniture and jewelry are also subject to probate.

Assets for which a beneficiary can be named, such as life insurance, annuities, and employee benefits pass to the named beneficiary at death without probate. Assets held in a living trust also avoid probate as do any assets held in joint tenancy.

Some states have simplified court proceedings in cases where there are assets subject to probate but these assets are being left to a surviving spouse.

COURT APPOINTMENT

If a probate is necessary, the first step is to file a petition with the court in the county in which the decedent lived at the time of death. The attorney will file this petition. After the petition is filed, a court hearing will be scheduled in approximately 30-60 days. In situations where business decisions have to made immediately, the court can appoint a "special administrator" to handle the estate and make any necessary decisions until the time of the hearing when an executor or administrator is appointed.

After the petition is filed, a notice regarding the court hearing must be published in a local paper. A notice of the hearing must also be mailed within a specified time (usually 15-30 days) to anyone named in the will as well as those who would by law normally inherit if there were no will. Depending on the state and the nature of the will, it might be necessary to obtain a statement from one of the witnesses to the will. Your attorney should guide you through all of these steps.

At the court hearing the will is "admitted to probate" and an executor or administrator is appointed. An executor is the person named in the decedent's will to handle his or her estate. This is often a surviving spouse, one or all of the children, another relative, or a friend. Several people can serve together as executors. An administrator is the person appointed by the court to handle the estate if there is no will. After someone is appointed as executor or administrator, he or she must file a special form, either a "letters testamentary" or a "letters of administration," indicating that he or she agrees to act as executor or administrator. When the executor or administrator is transferring assets or taking legal action, he or she will sometimes have to produce certified copies of these letters to prove that he or she indeed is the executor or administrator. Depending on the state and the nature of the will, the executor or administrator might have to post a surety bond. This is essentially an insurance policy insuring the estate if the executor or administrator steals from it or makes an error causing financial loss. The premium is paid out of the estate and might cost from $200 to several thousand dollars.

COLLECTING ASSETS

The executor or administrator collects all of the decedent's assets which are subject to probate. He or she does this by changing the title to these assets so that they are in his or her name as executor or administrator. The next step in most states is for an inventory to be made up itemizing all of these assets. Some states have a referee who assigns a fair market value as of the date of death to all of the non-cash assets in probate. Fees vary, but in some states the referee gets a fee of one dollar per $1,000 of the assets being appraised. An appraisal of the assets in probate is supposed to be filed with the court within a specified time of the appointment of the executor or administrator.

PAYING THE BILLS

Once appointed, the executor or administrator can start paying the bills. State laws vary, but in some states an executor or administrator can require creditors to file special forms called a creditor's claim. Sometimes the executor or administrator might reject a creditor's claim. There are specified time limits that vary from state to state regarding how long after death someone can file a claim, or how long a creditor has to sue an estate. Such claims or lawsuits are fairly rare.

SELLING ESTATE ASSETS

After being appointed, the executor or administrator and the attorney usually prepare a budget for the estate. This includes an estimate of the federal estate tax, the attorney's and executor's fees, administrative costs, any cash bequests in the will, and any debts or claims. If there isn't enough cash, then decisions have to be made regarding what assets to sell. Even if there is enough cash, for various reasons assets such as a home might be sold anyway. Depending on the state, court approval might be necessary before any asset can be sold. Or perhaps the executor or administrator can sell assets without court approval, although some states require that any beneficiary of the estate likely to be affected by the sale be notified in advance.

PAYING TAXES

The executor or administrator is responsible for paying all of the federal and state taxes owed by the estate and in some cases can be personally liable if the tax is not paid. Unless the executor or administrator is skilled in accounting, he or she probably shouldn't do the tax work alone. In some cases the attorney might handle it, or in others the accountant who handled the decedent's taxes before his or her death might handle it. If the decedent had over $1,500,000 or more in assets, depending on the year of death, a federal estate tax must be filed within nine months of the date of death. This amount increases from 2004 to 2010. Assets left to most charities or left to the decedent's spouse are not counted in this amount. A tax of 45-48% is payable on the amount of assets over $1,500,000. In addition to the federal estate tax, an income tax return has to be filed covering the period from January 1st until the date of death. The return is due April 15th of the following year. Any income which comes to the estate after the date of death must also be reported on a separate fiduciary or estate income tax return. Such returns can be filed on a fiscal year basis and not a calendar year basis. In addition to these taxes there might be real estate taxes on any property sold, sales tax if the estate includes a business selling a product, or even a gift tax if the decedent made a gift of over $11,000 to someone during the year of death.

CLOSING THE ESTATE

The estate can be closed once all of the assets have been inventoried, the period for filing creditor's claims has expired, all claims have been paid or resolved, any assets sold, and all taxes paid. A petition is filed with the court. The executor or administrator either turns in a detailed account of all receipts and disbursements or obtains a waiver of accounting from all of the estate beneficiaries. If there are no objections, the court orders the fees paid and the assets distributed. These assets can then be re-registered in the names of the beneficiaries.

EXECUTOR'S AND ATTORNEY'S FEES

Many states have statutory fees for the executor or administrator and the attorney. These are calculated as a percentage of the estate. The fees are generally calculated as a few percentage points on the first thousands of dollars of the estate, a lower percentage point on the next few thousands of dollars in the estate, and a still lower percentage point on the balance of the estate assets. The executor or administrator can waive part or all of his or her fees. He or she can also request extraordinary fees above these amounts.

In other states the attorney and executor receive a fee based on an hourly amount. In most cases, whether the fee is statutory or hourly, it will be substantial.

• PLAN AHEAD

Of all the *PLAN AHEAD* sections in this book, this is the most important. Probate takes time and costs money. With some careful estate planning, you can generally arrange things so that all of your assets, or at least a substantial portion of them, avoid probate.

Find an estate planning attorney now and arrange your assets to minimize or eliminate probate. Remember that any attorney's fees which you have to pay now will be paid back many times over by the money your loved ones will save by avoiding probate costs after your death. Discuss your plans with your loved ones and decide who would be the best executor of the will. If possible, try to work out any potential disagreements about who will get what, now, before your death. Any of the steps involved in a probate can be prolonged while relatives fight amongst themselves over the estate. It's almost always better to discuss these things openly and honestly now, before your death, and minimize hard feelings, family fighting, and legal fees later on.

TRANSFERRING ASSETS

Not all estates go through probate. Nevertheless when someone dies, there are some things which have to be done to get the assets transferred into the name of the person or persons legally entitled to them. If assets are in joint tenancy, the assets must be transferred and put into the name of the surviving joint tenant or tenants. If life insurance is payable to a named beneficiary, the beneficiary must submit the necessary claim form to the insurance company. Many things have to be done to have assets legally transferred even though these assets do not go through the probate process.

TERMINATION OF JOINT TENANCY

Assets in joint tenancy avoid probate and automatically go to the surviving joint tenant or tenants. It is important to check if the words "joint tenants," "joint tenancy," "JTWROS," "JTTen," or similar wording is used. Property in the name of two or more people with the word "and" or "or" between the names is **not** necessarily held in joint tenancy. To determine if assets are in joint tenancy, you need to get a copy of the deed to real estate, stock and bond certificates, mutual fund statements, brokerage firm statements, and bank books or statements.

To terminate joint tenancy and put the asset into the name of the surviving joint tenant or tenants, the only legal document required by most states is a certified copy of the death certificate. Other documents which are needed vary with the asset involved.

Real Estate

In addition to recording the necessary documents, there may be a number of other non-legal matters to accomplish. Tenants have to be notified of the death and about the payment of future rent. If there has been a homeowner's exemption on the property and it cannot legally continue, the county assessor or tax collector must be notified. The insurance company which handles the home ownership insurance should be notified and the policy changed to reflect the change in ownership. Any lenders should also be notified to change their records to reflect the death of the joint tenant.

In many states, property is reassessed and taxes increased when there is a change of ownership. This includes situations when someone dies. However, in some cases the spouse, and possibly the children, are exempt from this process. If there is a reassessment of the property, special forms must usually be filled out and submitted with an affidavit or other document terminating the joint tenancy.

Notes Secured by Deed of Trust or Mortgage

Sometimes the decedent was a payee under a deed of trust or mortgage. The decedent had lent money and secured the loan by a deed of trust or mortgage on the real estate. There are two documents involved—a note and a deed of trust or mortgage. The note is not recorded, but the deed of trust or mortgage is recorded. If the note and deed of trust or mortgage are in joint tenancy, no action is necessary with regard to the note, other than notifying the payer or payers to make payment to the surviving joint tenant or tenants. With regard to the deed of trust or mortgage, it is only necessary to record a real estate form, with a certified copy of the death certificate. Since this is only a deed of trust or mortgage, there is no change with regard to the real estate taxes.

Notes

A note not secured by deed of trust or mortgage which is in joint tenancy can easily be handled by advising the payer of the death of one of the parties and providing the payer with a certified copy of the death certificate. No legal action or recording is necessary. When the note is paid off, it is marked "paid" by the surviving joint tenant and delivered to the payer. It is important to verify the balance on the note as of the date of death.

Securities

Many people own stocks, registered bonds, bearer bonds, mutual funds, brokerage accounts, treasury direct account, or other assets termed "securities." To terminate these assets, the basic document needed is a certified copy of the death certificate. First, it must be determined if the asset is in joint tenancy. The words "joint tenancy," "JTWROS," or "jt. ten." must be on the certificate, fund statement or brokerage statement. To transfer stock certificates or registered bonds, the certificates must be returned to the transfer agent. The transfer agent is normally a bank. The transfer agent is usually listed on the certificate but may have changed since the certificate was issued. To find the transfer agent one can generally check with a local brokerage firm or the public library, which has a directory of such institutions. After the death of a person, the certificate is sent in with a short letter to the transfer agent, indicating the transfer and giving the name, address, and social security number of the new registered owner. A certified copy of the death certificate, affidavit of domicile, and stock power usually must also be sent in. Many transfer agents also require Internal Revenue Service form W-9, certifying the person's social security number. The documents should be sent by certified mail, return receipt required, and insured for approximately 10 to 15% of the value, to cover costs if the certificates are lost.

If the decedent was a joint tenant on a brokerage account, the only document the survivor will need will be a certified copy of the death certificate. The brokerage firm will complete other forms needed, and this will allow the transfer of all assets in the brokerage account. If a brokerage firm is holding 50 issues of stock in a joint tenancy brokerage account, one death certificate will transfer all 50 companies on their books.

If a mutual fund is involved, normally no certificates are outstanding, and an irrevocable stock power, certified copy of the death certificate, and affidavit of domicile are sufficient to transfer the asset. In many cases, the fund may also require a new application by the surviving joint tenant.

If the decedent owned bearer bonds, since these are not registered, no action or probate is necessary if other assets are not subject to probate. If other assets are probated, then the bearer bonds will also be subject to the probate proceedings.

Bank and Savings and Loan Accounts

If a bank or savings and loan account is in joint tenancy, it generally passes to the surviving joint tenants at death. The only document required is a certified copy of the death certificate. Many financial institutions do not require a copy of the death certificate, since any one of the joint tenants could have drawn out the funds during the lifetime of the decedent. If the funds are in a certificate of deposit or time certificate, some institutions will allow the certificate to be canceled early without penalty if one of the parties on the certificate dies. Many accounts which are in joint tenancy are kept open for a period of time and the funds are later withdrawn by the surviving joint tenant. This is perfectly legal and is permissible.

Automobiles

For an automobile, motorcycle, trailer or small boat to be in joint tenancy, the certificate of ownership issued by the state Department of Motor Vehicles, sometimes referred to as the "pink slip," must have the parties' names with the word "or" on it. The surviving joint tenant can transfer the vehicle with the local Department of Motor Vehicles office by submitting the certificate of ownership and registration certificate for the vehicle and paying a small fee. It is not necessary to transfer a vehicle in joint tenancy since any one of the owners alone can sign off and transfer it. If John and Mary Doe own their car in joint tenancy and John dies, Mary can later sell or transfer the vehicle by her signature alone. If Mary dies before transferring, the vehicle would still pass by her will. You can find out what documents are needed by a phone call to the local motor vehicle office.

Income Tax Refunds

In the year of death, it is possible for the decedent and the surviving spouse to still file a joint income tax return. Generally, it is advantageous for the surviving spouse to do this, since the tax will normally be lower than if separate returns were filed. If a joint return is filed, and a refund is due, it passes automatically to the surviving spouse, and not to the decedent's estate. This is true even if there is a probate proceeding. If there is no surviving spouse and no probate, whoever is legally entitled to the refund can file Internal Revenue Service form 1310 to obtain the refund in his or her name. If there is no spouse but there is a probate, the refund will go to the executor or administrator of the estate.

Oil Royalties

Mineral rights such as oil royalties are treated like real property in terms of terminating joint tenancy. After the title to the mineral interest is recorded, a copy of the recorded real estate form needs to be sent to the oil company to have them change their records.

Other Assets

Other assets may be in joint tenancy. To transfer these assets, the issuing organization is contacted and furnished a certified copy of the death certificate. The organization such as the bank, stock transfer agent, or general partner will advise the surviving joint tenant what documents will be required to put the asset in the survivor's name.

Creditor's Rights against Surviving Joint Tenant

The general rule is that if assets are in joint tenancy, the surviving joint tenant is not liable for unsecured debts of the decedent. There may be some liability if the surviving joint tenant is the surviving spouse and the debt was for medical or living costs. Secured debts such as a note secured by a deed of trust on real property follow the asset. If the surviving joint tenant signed a contract or document, such as the funeral contract after death, then the survivor will be liable.

Tenants by the Entireties

Some states allow a husband and wife to hold title in their names as "tenants by the entireties." This basically is like a joint tenancy registration, so the property passes to the surviving spouse on the death of the first spouse. A real estate form and a certified copy of the death certificate are generally the only legal documents needed to change title.

BENEFICIARY DESIGNATION ASSETS

Assets not subject to probate also include assets where the decedent was allowed to designate a beneficiary. At death these assets pass to the designated beneficiary. The beneficiary must submit a certified copy of the death certificate and a claim form to the insurance company or trustees of the employee plan.

Life Insurance

A life insurance policy is a contract whereby the insurance company agrees to pay a certain sum upon the death of the named insured. The amount is payable to the person, persons, or organization designated as the beneficiary. John Doe takes out a $100,000 policy and designates his wife as the beneficiary. Upon his death, the company will pay $100,000 to his wife. If the primary beneficiary does not survive, then the benefits will be paid to the secondary beneficiary, if any. If John Doe's wife dies ahead of him, and his two children are named as the secondary beneficiaries, they will then receive the $100,000. If no beneficiary survives or if no beneficiaries are listed, then the insurance proceeds will be paid to the insured person's estate, and pass by his or her will.

To receive benefits after the death of the insured, the insurance company should be immediately contacted. They will normally send out a short form for completion by the beneficiary. This claim form, a certified copy of the death certificate and, in some cases, the original policy will be mailed to the insurance company. The company will then pay the proceeds within approximately 60 days of receipt of the documents.

The insurance company will deduct from the proceeds any loans which the decedent took out against the policy prior to death, but will add to the proceeds any supplemental insurance, postmortem dividends or other benefits due plus interest if the proceeds are not paid within approximately 30 days of the submission of the claim forms. Life insurance proceeds are not subject to income tax (except for any interest paid after death), but the proceeds are normally subject to federal estate tax.

Single Premium Deferred Annuity

Many people take out a single premium deferred annuity, as an investment. This is quite different from a life insurance policy. Here, John Doe gives his insurance company $100,000, which is invested in this single premium deferred annuity. It earns interest and John Doe does not have to pay income tax on it until he withdraws funds from the insurance company. Upon his death, if he is the annuitant, the $100,000 plus accrued interest is paid to the named beneficiary. As with life insurance, a claim form is submitted with the policy and a certified copy of the death certificate to the insurance company, and the proceeds are paid in a lump sum to the named beneficiary. Here, the entire proceeds of the annuity are taxable for federal estate tax purposes, but the accrued income over and above the amount originally put into the policy is also taxable for income tax purposes.

Corporate Benefits

Many people are covered by some sort of employee benefit plan. This may be a pension plan, a profit sharing plan, a stock purchase plan or some other type of corporation plan. Again, the employee designates a beneficiary to receive any benefits which are payable at death. The named beneficiary submits a claim form and a certified copy of the employee's death certificate to the trustees of the plan. The benefits are payable to the beneficiary in cash, or in stock, or other assets of the plan. Because of the nature of these plans, the amount of benefits due in many cases cannot be paid until after the end of the current plan year. The beneficiary may not receive the full amount of benefits for up to a year after death, or in a few cases, even longer.

The benefits payable under a corporate plan are subject to federal estate tax. They are also subject to income tax. Because of special income tax treatment of lump sum distributions from a corporation plan, a beneficiary should check with a knowledgeable tax person about the taxability of the benefits and the tax options available before filing a claim. If the spouse is the named beneficiary, he or she can roll over the benefits income tax free to a new IRA account.

Keogh Plan

Many self-employed individuals and their employees are covered by a self-employed retirement plan, called an HR-10 or Keogh plan. As with a corporation plan, the employee names a beneficiary and, at death, the amount set aside for the employee is paid in a lump sum to that beneficiary. At death the beneficiary submits a claim form and a certified copy of the death certificate to the trustees of the plan.

The benefits under a Keogh plan are taxed essentially the same as the benefits under a corporation plan. Many corporation and Keogh plans have a provision that if no beneficiary is designated, the benefits are automatically paid to the nearest relatives in a certain listed order.

In other plans, if no beneficiary is designated or survives the employee, the benefits are paid to the decedent's estate and are subject to probate.

Individual Retirement Account

Many people open Individual Retirement Accounts. These are accounts where the person may contribute up to a certain amount each year and, in some cases, get an income tax deduction for the amount contributed. At the time of the death of the covered participant, the benefits are paid, as with a corporate or Keogh plan, to a named beneficiary. The beneficiary submits the necessary claim form to the trustee or trustees of the plan along with a certified copy of the death certificate, and the benefits are paid in a lump sum. If the primary beneficiary is deceased but a secondary beneficiary survives, the amount in the IRA is paid to the secondary beneficiary. If no beneficiary is named or none survives the participant, then the benefits pass to the participant's estate and are subject to probate.

Individuals who retire from a corporation can elect to receive their benefits and pay income tax on them, or roll over the amount received within sixty days to an IRA account and not pay income tax at that time. Once a rollover is elected, the party is then subject to the income tax rules for the IRA, which are sometimes less generous than those for a corporate plan. If a spouse is the beneficiary of an IRA plan, then upon the death of the participant, the spouse (but only the spouse) may also elect to roll over the amount received to a new IRA account and not pay income tax on it at that time.

When a person who has an IRA account dies and the beneficiary files a claim form, he or she receives the benefits and they are subject to income tax. A beneficiary does not have to file a claim immediately, since the IRA law provides that a beneficiary must receive the benefits (and pay income tax) or start drawing the benefits within a certain period of time. (The time period varies depending on several factors.) IRA benefits are also subject to estate tax (although the spouse is exempt). The fair market value of the IRA account must be added to all other assets the decedent owned.

The rules for withdrawing funds from IRA, Keogh, and corporate accounts are very complicated. With many benefits, the benefits can be withdrawn over the individual's lifetime. Before filing a claim or withdrawing any benefits, the beneficiary should get advice from a knowledgeable tax professional.

LIVING TRUST ASSETS

Many people set up a living trust to avoid probate at death. If John Doe wishes to avoid probate, John Doe can set up a living trust by having an attorney prepare a trust agreement or trust declaration. Assets are then transferred and registered in the name of the trustee: "John Doe, Trustee of the John Doe Living Trust, dated May 10, 1996." Upon the death of John Doe, the trust may terminate or the trust may continue for another beneficiary such as one or more of the children.

The trust agreement will name a successor trustee, such as the son, Sam Doe, to become trustee upon the death of John Doe. The son will then have to contact each bank, stock transfer agent or other party and transfer the assets into his name, "Sam Doe, Trustee of the John Doe Living Trust, dated May 10, 1996." This is true even if the trust terminates. The successor trustee will have to register the assets in his or her name, and then re-register them in the name of the parties who receive them. To transfer the assets the successor trustee will need for each asset a certified copy of the death certificate and a certified copy of the trust agreement (a copy of the trust certified as being a correct copy by a bank, stock broker, or attorney).

The assets in a living trust are controlled by the trust documents and not by the decedent's will. However, assets which are not registered in the trust's name and which are in the decedent's name alone are controlled by the will.

PENSION BENEFITS

If the decedent was receiving a pension at death, the pension may continue to be paid to another party, such as the spouse. The pension administrator needs to be contacted and if the pension continues, various forms will have to be filled out. The only legal document needed is a certified copy of the death certificate.

TRUSTEE BANK AND SAVINGS AND LOAN ACCOUNTS

Many people open an account at a bank, savings and loan association, or credit union in their name as trustee for someone else: "Jane Doe, Trustee for Martha Doe." Here, there is no formal trust, but only a way of taking title to the account. This is sometimes called a "Totten" trust. Sometimes assets are registered as "Jane Doe ATF Martha Doe," with the ATF standing for "as trustee for." At death the account passes to the named beneficiary. Martha Doe would only need a certified copy of the death certificate of Jane Doe to collect the funds in the account. Again, the funds are fully taxable for federal estate tax purposes.

If an account is in the name of "John Doe and Jane Doe, Trustees for Martha Doe," and Jane Doe dies, the account is treated as a joint tenancy account and passes to John Doe. He would need a certified copy of the death certificate to collect the funds. If he wished, he could terminate the account and change the registration. If he did not change it, then upon his later death, the funds would pass to Martha Doe with a certified copy of his death certificate. If the account is a term certificate of deposit, it may be canceled early without penalty upon the death of the owner.

CHARITABLE REMAINDER TRUST

Some individuals and couples set up a special type of irrevocable trust called a "charitable remainder trust," in which the assets ultimately pass to a charity. Payments are made to the individual or couple and then may terminate at death or continue for a period of years or even the lifetime of another individual. As with a pension, the trustee of the trust needs to be contacted and provided with a certified copy of the death certificate. Various papers or internal forms will probably have to be completed.

P.O.D. REGISTRATION ASSETS

Bank, savings and loan, and credit union accounts may also be taken in someone's name payable on death or "P.O.D." to another. An account in the name of "Jane Doe, P.O.D. Martha Doe" passes to Martha Doe upon Jane Doe's death. Again, a certified copy of the death certificate is all that is needed to transfer the funds at death.

United States Savings Bonds are another example of an asset which can be set up to be payable at death. A bond could be registered in the name of "Jane Doe, P.O.D. Martha Doe." Upon the death of Jane Doe, Martha could surrender the bonds to the federal government with a certified copy of the death certificate and receive the proceeds from the redemption. The proceeds are subject to income tax on the interest which has accumulated since the bonds were purchased. They are also subject to estate tax.

T.O.D. REGISTRATION ASSETS

T.O.D. stands for "transfer on death and is used for brokerage accounts, stock registration, and mutual funds. An account, stock, or fund registered in the name of "John Doe, T.O.D. Mary Smith" passes to Mary Smith on John Doe's death. As in the case of a P.O.D. registration, a certified copy of the death certificate is all that is needed to transfer the security at death.

This type of registration can only be used for securities, and only if the brokerage firm, mutual fund, or stock registration agent allows this type of registration.

SPOUSAL CONFIRMATION PROCEEDINGS

In some states, when either husband or wife dies and leaves assets to the other spouse, no probate is necessary. In some cases a simplified court proceeding, frequently referred to as a "Spousal Confirmation Proceeding," is used. Husband or wife may own separate property in that person's name alone, or assets may be owned by both spouses in their names as "community property." Not being registered in joint tenancy, this property would normally require probate. To use a Spousal Confirmation Proceeding, the assets must pass outright to the spouse.

If a trust or a formal life estate has been set up, probate will be required.

You need to find out if this procedure can be used in your state. If not, the assets may have to go through probate before they can pass to the spouse.

SMALL ESTATE

Many states have passed laws to avoid probating small estates. Over the years, the amount that can pass without probate has been increased. The amount varies from state to state. If the assets are below this minimum amount, no probate is necessary. Only the gross value of the assets is used and the liabilities are not taken into account in computing the minimum amount. Many times a person dies thinking that everything is in joint tenancy. Sometimes assets such as cars, bank accounts, or stock are missed. As long as the assets that normally would be subject to probate are worth less than the state's minimum allowable amount, this provision can be used. If more than the minimum amount is in the decedent's name, all of the assets in the decedent's name are subject to probate, not just the amount over the minimum figure.

As noted above, this minimum amount varies from state to state. It can be as low as $5,000 or as high as $100,000.

• PLAN AHEAD

There are few things more important in planning your estate than knowing what your assets are and how title to these assets is held. Keep an up-to-date list of all your assets that includes information regarding how title is held. Don't guess as to how title is held. Physically review each document. If you're still not sure, ask someone at the financial institution. Update the list annually and keep the list at home. Make sure that your loved ones know where the list is.

IF THE DECEDENT HAD A TRUST

Many people have living trusts these days. What happens when a person with a living trust dies? One important step is to determine what assets are in the trust and what assets are not. If the person planned carefully, most large assets, such as real property, bank, savings and loan, and brokerage accounts will be in the trust. You need to check the title to each item. Items in the trust are generally registered as something like "John Doe, Trustee of the John Doe Living Trust, dated June 6, 1993."

What happens next depends on the trust. All trusts should have a named successor trustee. When a married couple has a trust done, in most (but not all) cases the surviving spouse will be named as the successor trustee. In other cases, a child, some or all of the children, or fiduciary (such as a bank) might be named as the successor trustee. The trust may terminate at the death of the initial trust creator, in which case the money and assets in the trust will be distributed to named beneficiaries. Or in some cases the trust may continue on, perhaps until a named beneficiary reaches a stated age or until a named beneficiary dies.

Another important step is to find out who the successor trustee is. Managing the trust is the successor trustee's responsibility. He or she should probably contact an attorney so that the attorney can advise him or her of the responsibilities involved. Acting as the trustee can involve a lot of work. Sometimes someone named as the trustee will feel that it is too much work, and will decline to serve. In such cases a new trustee will be named. In most states this will require a court hearing, although such hearings are usually mere formalities. If an alternate is named in the original living trust document or an amendment, that person can serve. If there is no named alternate trustee, the named successor trustee can frequently nominate someone, although this will probably require a court hearing as well as the approval of the beneficiaries of the trust. Again, this will probably require a court hearing for approval and possibly require the posting of a surety bond, with annual premiums.

Once someone is named successor trustee, he or she will have the trust assets registered in his or her name as the trustee of the trust. This will usually involve dealing with each bank, savings and loan, brokerage firm, stock transfer agent, and person or institution handling other accounts individually. In most cases a certified death certificate will be required, as well as a legal document such as an affidavit, and perhaps other documents. Depending on the number of assets involved, this might take quite a bit of time.

The full duties of a trustee fall beyond the scope of this book. Suffice it to say that it will probably be time consuming and that you should almost certainly get competent legal advice. A trust beneficiary who feels that things aren't being done the way he or she would like will quite possibly question your conduct as trustee. You need to be sure that you perform your duties as trustee in a proper legal manner with no personal financial liability.

• PLAN AHEAD

Generally speaking, if you are worth $1,500,000 or more, or will be worth that much shortly, you might want to think about getting a living trust. With a living trust a husband and wife can eliminate or save significantly on the amount of federal estate tax the heirs will pay when both parties die. For a couple or a single person, assets in a living trust avoid probate. If you have a living trust, make sure that the named successor trustee or trustees know who they are and that they have copies of the living trust and any amendments.

IF THE DECEDENT WAS A TRUSTEE, EXECUTOR, OR FIDUCIARY

If the decedent was acting as a trustee, executor, administrator, conservator, guardian, or as a fiduciary in another capacity, the assets handled in that capacity were not owned by him or her. It will be necessary to get someone else to handle these assets and to take over this job. This will usually require a court hearing. It is up to the decedent's executor, estate attorney, or nearest relatives if there is no executor to assist with the transfer of assets to the new fiduciary, and an accounting of funds may be required.

It is important to identify assets in the decedent's name as executor, trustee, or fiduciary. To identify such assets, check bank statements, brokerage reports, statements from mutual funds, and stock certificates to see if any of these are in the name of an estate, trust, guardianship, or conservatorship. You should also examine copies of the most recent income tax return filed prior to the decedent's death to identify any assets that are in an estate, trust, guardianship, or conservatorship.

If there has been a court proceeding, there will be a court file for the estate, trust, conservatorship, or guardianship. You should review any such file and obtain copies of any relevant documents which the decedent didn't have in his or her records. In cases such as these, there generally has been an attorney advising the decedent. The attorney should be consulted regarding who has the right to act as successor fiduciary and what the procedure is to name a successor.

Many people serve as custodians for children or grandchildren under what is called the Uniform Gift to Minors Act or Uniform Transfers to Minors Act. (every state has one or the other.) Normally, only one person at a time can serve as custodian. If the custodian dies prior to the termination and distribution of the assets, another custodian takes over. If paperwork has not been done, it may be necessary to go to court to have a successor custodian appointed.

• PLAN AHEAD

If you are acting as a trustee, executor, administrator, conservator, guardian, or as a fiduciary in another capacity, you should be aware of any provisions for alternate fiduciaries. Make sure that your loved ones are aware of these provisions so that at the time of your death they won't be caught up in the intricacies of other people's financial affairs as well as your own. Make sure they have the name and number of any attorney advising you on these matters. Make sure that they have any documents which might be necessary to expedite the naming of a successor trustee, executor, administrator, conservator, guardian, or other fiduciary.

It is also important to keep accurate financial records. If you are the executor of someone else's estate and you die 18 months into the probate, someone else is probably going to have to file a detailed accounting as to all the receipts and disbursements for the period in which you were executor. This can be extremely time consuming if you haven't kept accurate records and may even require the services of an accountant who might be paid out of the assets of the estate or trust or paid out of your assets if you have not kept the required records.

If you are a custodian under your state's Uniform Gift to Minors Act or Uniform Transfers to Minors Act, check the procedure for naming your successor upon your death. If no successor is named, a court proceeding may be necessary to have someone appointed.

WRONGFUL DEATH ACTION

If the decedent died as the result of someone's negligence, it may be possible for the decedent's spouse, children or other relatives to bring a "wrongful death action." This action is for the emotional distress brought about by the loss of a loved one and also includes monetary damages for the financial loss of support and income which the person would have received if the decedent had not died.

If you believe that you might have grounds for a wrongful death action, you will need to contact an attorney who specializes in this area of law. There is a limited period of time in which you can file an action for wrongful death, (frequently one year from the date of death) so you should consult an attorney who specializes in this area of law fairly soon after the decedent's death, generally within a few weeks at most.

The person or organization which caused the death may be insured, even if the person or organization has very few assets. If an automobile was involved in the death, the owner of the vehicle or the employer (if the vehicle was operated by a business) may have liability.

Most people are unaware that if a wrongful death action is successful, anyone who paid out money because of the decedent's death has a right to reimbursement. Suppose a man is struck by a drunk driver and is hospitalized but then dies in the hospital. His medical bills, totaling $275,000 are paid by Medicare and supplemental medical insurance. The relatives settle with the drunk driver's insurance company for $300,000. Medicare and the decedent's supplemental insurance company each have a subrogation right, or a right to be reimbursed for their share of the $275,000 payment. Sometimes people sue and spend several years in court only to find that they have to give most of the money they receive to others, such as Medicare or a supplemental insurance company.

If a minor is involved in the lawsuit, a court appointed guardian may be necessary to represent the minor in connection with the suit.

If the death was accidental, the attorney who advises family members can usually refer them to a specialist who handles wrongful death actions. Sometimes when a person dies in a hospital or convalescent hospital from "natural" causes, there is the possibility that the death was related to lack of proper medical care. In such cases, an autopsy may be important and may be ordered by relatives even when it is not legally required by the government.

Lawsuits can be very intensive and last for a long period of time—sometimes up to five years. However, if there is any question as to the cause of death, this area should at least be discussed and explored. In many cases the family may decide not to pursue a wrongful death action even when there might be a chance of recovery because of the time factors, the emotional strain involved, and the chance that a portion of the money might be paid out to an insurance company or Medicare.

FINANCIAL
CONCERNS

Financial concerns come into play after the decedent's death. Sometimes the decedent has carefully planned his or her estate so that only a quick consultation with an attorney or accountant will be necessary and a few forms will need to be signed. However, in many cases the decedent has done no planning at all, and the financial situation is a mess which might take months or years to straighten out.

One of the first things to consider is incoming bills. Can these be paid? Who can write checks? Are there only a few easily paid bills, or are there thousands of dollars of medical costs? Did the decedent run his or her own business? Is there someone who can manage the business, whether for the short run or the long run?

There is the issue of valuing the assets. A federal estate tax return will have to be filed if the decedent's assets are worth more than $1,500,000 to 3,500,000, depending on the year of death, and it is possible that some federal estate tax will be due. To file the return you will have to know how much the decedent's assets are worth. There is the issue of getting casualty insurance for tangible assets such as real or personal property.

What are you going to do about social security and other payments? Can checks issued after death be cashed, or must they be returned to the issuing organization? Who has the right to enter the safe deposit box?

Depending on the decedent's work situation, there might be the issue of retirement and annuity benefits, pension, profit sharing, IRA and other benefits. Also, the insurance company which issued the life insurance has to be contacted and dealt with.

As this book is being written, the state of health care and medical insurance is in a state of flux and change. Even if American health care and insurance come to operate more smoothly and efficiently in the coming years, you will still have to deal with whatever medical bills may arise and the insurance situation related to the decedent. As more and more people die in hospitals or in managed health care facilities, large medical bills and complicated insurance situations will be faced by more and more survivors.

If there is a probate, many of these concerns will be handled by the executor or administrator. But in a majority of cases there won't be a probate (and even in cases where there is one, there will probably be assets not subject to probate). In these situations the decisions will fall to the nearest surviving relatives. (And in most cases the executor or administrator is one of the nearest surviving relatives.)

Nevertheless, the person who is the executor or administrator is not always someone who inherits under the will. Nor are the people who inherit under the will always the designated beneficiaries of life insurance policies or IRA benefits. If the decedent has planned well, there will be no major surprises. But it is not unknown for someone to die and for his wife to discover that an insurance policy or IRA account still lists a previous wife as the named beneficiary. Once the decedent is dead, the designation can't be changed.

Be prepared to spend a lot of time with these financial concerns. Many times the survivors express the wish that they could just finish up all this business. These matters will probably take several months to sort out. And while it is possible that you are independently wealthy and don't care much what happens, it is more likely that you will need to deal with these properly in order to contribute to your own financial future.

PAYING THE BILLS

One of the first legal concerns after someone dies is the question of who is going to pay the bills. If you or someone else is a co-signer on the decedent's accounts, there is no problem. But if there is no co-signer and bills are coming in, someone has to pay them. Even if there is a probate, it will take 30-60 days to have an executor or administrator appointed. Who pays the bills in the meantime?

You should determine all of the bank, savings and loan, and credit union accounts which the decedent owned at the time of his or her death and the following information about each.

- Name of Institution
- Branch Address
- Type of Account
- Current Balance
- Title to Account

You should determine whether these accounts were in the decedent's name alone, in joint tenancy with someone, or in a trustee or P.O.D. designation, so that the account passed to a named beneficiary at death. To find out this information you need to contact the financial institution.

Many times financial institutions will not give anyone information until an executor or administrator has been appointed and the institution has a certified copy of the court appointment. If this is the case, review the last bank statement. Normally the statement or passbook shows how title is held to the account, as well as the account balance. If you're not sure what accounts the decedent held, check Schedule B of the decedent's last federal income tax return. This should itemize any accounts in the decedent's name. If the decedent had bills which aren't going to be paid until after a probate is begun, you need to contact the various creditors and advise them of the delay in payment.

If the decedent gave someone a power of attorney to sign on his accounts before death, this power of attorney legally terminates at death. The agent under the power of attorney cannot sign any further checks.

If information is needed, you should review the last bank statements. Normally the statement or passbook shows how title is held, as well as the account balance. If you are unsure what bank accounts the decedent had, you should review Schedule B of the decedent's last income tax return, which should itemize these accounts.

•   PLAN AHEAD

If you are the only signer on a bank account, make some sort of plan for paying the bills after your death. This is especially important if you are the sole proprietor of a business. This might mean having the bills paid out of another account, one on which someone else is a signer or co-signer. If you are the sole owner of a business and this is impossible, you should consider having someone else as co-signer on your business account. Even if you intend that the business cease to exist after your death, life will still be much easier for your survivors if you make some allowance for paying the bills.

CONTINUING BUSINESS AFTER DEATH

If the decedent owned a business, who continues the business after death? This is extremely important if the business was one where the decedent was the sole owner. If the business was a professional practice, such as a legal firm, medical or dental practice, engineering or other firm, certain restrictions on ownership and transfer apply.

If there are several owners, there may be a buy-sell agreement which requires the other owners to buy the decedent's share of the business under a set formula or value. Many times this is funded with life insurance.

If the decedent was the sole owner then there are a number of immediate considerations. Who can sign on business bank accounts? Are there employees who have to be paid? Who can or will continue the business operation?

Normally it is a good idea to talk to the firm's accountant and attorney as soon as possible after death to determine what action must or should be taken. What action needs to be taken depends on many factors, one of which is the type of the business.

A *sole proprietorship* is a business owned by one person and usually operated under a fictitious business name. Generally, only the executor or administrator can handle the account of a sole proprietorship after the owner's death.

A *corporation* is run by a board of directors who elect officers to sign checks and run the day-to-day business. If the president is the only signer on the corporation bank accounts, the board of directors can immediately elect a new president. In some small corporations, one person owns all of the stock and is the sole director and sole officer. Whoever legally takes charge of the stock can elect a new director and new officer who can then sign on the accounts. If there is more than one shareholder, the shareholder holding more than fifty percent of the stock controls.

A *subchapter S corporation* is a corporation which has all of the income taxed annually to its shareholders rather than to the corporation. Getting someone to sign on the account would be handled in the same way as it would in a regular corporation.

A *limited liability corporation* is a corporation that is taxed like a partnership. Again, getting someone to sign on the account would be handled in the same way as it would in a regular corporation.

A *partnership* can be either a general or limited partnership.

A *general partnership* consists of two or more people, corporations, or other partnerships and is handled by a managing general partner. Upon one partner's death, the partnership agreement provides what happens to the deceased partner's share: whether it passes by his or her will, is purchased by the other partners, or is treated some other way. If the managing general partner dies, the surviving partners generally elect a new one.

A *limited partnership* is run by a general partner or partners with investors who are limited partners but who have no say in the operation of the partnership. Upon the death of a general partner, the partnership agreement provides what happens. A new general partner is either named in the agreement or is elected by all of the partners. The general partner's share of ownership passes to his estate.

One extremely important question is the value of the business. If there is an estate tax due, there will be an estate tax valuation of the business which will establish a new cost basis for income tax purposes. Knowing what the owner thought the business to be worth is often of little help in such situations. Typically, a business owner will wildly overestimate the value of the business. Once he or she is dead, the survivors, aware of the tax ramifications, will wildly underestimate the value of the business.

In such situations, the business's accountant is generally the person to turn to. He or she will also be aware of the sorts of factors the Internal Revenue Service considers when valuing a business. These include the market price of similar businesses, the history of the business, the outlook for the business and the industry in general, the book value, earnings capacity, and overall financial condition of the business, the dividend paying capacity of the business, any prior sales of business ownership by other owners, and any intangible value, such as goodwill. The business has a name and reputation. Will this die with the owner (or one of the owners) or will it continue on? In many cases the accountant or attorney will recommend using a specialized appraisal firm to help ascertain the value of the business.

SELLING THE BUSINESS

In some cases the survivors want to sell the business after the decedent's death. If it is sold within a year of the death, the sales price can generally be used as the value for tax purposes. If the business is sold after the one year period, the Internal Revenue Service may still consider this the value, or it may want to look at other factors and assign a different value. If the decedent owned a minority interest in the business (less than 50%) the Internal Revenue Service allows a discount involving the decedent's share of the value of the business.

In cases where there are several owners, such as in a general partnership or corporation, there may be a buy-sell agreement under which the remaining owners can (or in some cases must) buy the deceased owner's share in the business for either a pre-set price or a formula based price. If the business is a limited liability company or corporation, another option would be to have the company or corporation purchase the decedent's share of the business rather than to have the other shareholders buy it. In such cases there is usually a similar buy-sell agreement.

If there is no buy-sell agreement and family members do not want to continue the business, what happens? Depending on the business, there might be a major competitor or national chain that would be interested. Or there might be a key employee, or group of key employees who are capable of running the business and are interested in buying it.

If there is no buy-sell agreement, the decedent's will or trust controls whom the decedent's share of the business goes to. While most family members will probably have strong opinions regarding what should be done with the business, it is up to the person or people who actually inherit the business or share of the business to decide what is to be done. The following are some very general observations regarding what might happen to different types of businesses.

Depending on the nature of the business, a sole proprietorship may have to be terminated simply because no one wants to buy it. How much did the business depend on the decedent? If the answer is "almost entirely," then it will probably be impossible to sell it. On the other hand, there are sole proprietorships that do have value and that can continue on after the owner's death.

An interest in a limited partnership is usually left to someone by a will or trust. This is often more of an investment than a business interest and generally cannot be sold.

A general partner's interest depends on the partnership agreement. Again, what can be done with this interest is usually controlled by any buy-sell agreements and the partnership agreement itself. If there are no provisions to cover selling the decedent's share, it may be possible to amend the partnership agreement to allow the decedent's heirs to sell their interest.

If there is no buy-sell agreement, there are generally no restrictions on selling all of or an interest in a corporation, subchapter S corporation, or limited liability company. Again, the decedent's will or trust controls what happens to his or her share. If the decedent owned a majority interest in the corporation, subchapter S corporation, or limited liability company, the control of the business will pass to the person or persons named in the decedent's will or trust.

Again, these are only very broad generalizations. When someone who owns a business dies, you should see his or her accountant and attorney to discuss what needs to be done and what the options are.

• PLAN AHEAD

If you run your own business, make sure that there is some provision so that the business can carry on after your death. If you are the sole signer on the bank accounts, make sure that your loved ones know how to proceed to get someone else to sign. Let them know whether the business is a corporation, general partnership, or limited partnership. Make sure they know where any relevant corporation documents or partnership agreements are stored so that these can be consulted by an attorney. If you own a business along with other people and there is a buy-sell agreement, make sure that your loved ones know of the existence of the agreement and have at least a rough idea of its terms.

VALUING THE ASSETS

The assets of the decedent need to be valued as of the date of death. Assets get a new value for income tax purposes when someone dies. If a federal estate tax return is filed, the new value is the value listed on the federal estate tax return. This is either the fair market value as of the date of death or six months after the date of death. If no federal estate tax return is required, the new value is the fair market value as of the date of death.

This valuation is needed to determine if a federal estate tax return is due. If the value of all of the decedent's assets is over $1,500,000 to 3,500,000 at the date of death, a federal estate tax return is due nine months from the date of death. If it is under this amount, no federal estate tax return is due.

As long as the decedent was a United States citizen or permanent resident, all assets, even those in another country, must be valued and reported. These assets might include real property, stocks, bonds, bank accounts, life insurance, IRA accounts, company pension benefits, cars, furniture, loans to family members, and unexercised stock options.

The value of each asset is the "fair market value" as of the date of death. This is the value that would be obtained if the assets were sold on the date of death. The Internal Revenue Service has regulations regarding the valuation of some assets.

For stocks and bonds which are traded on a regular market, the value is the average between the high and low on the date of death. If the decedent died on a weekend or holiday, the value is the average of the high and low on both the last trading day before death and the first trading day after death. For mutual funds, the fair market value is the redemption value as of the date of death or the last business day before death if the decedent died on a weekend or holiday. For real estate, a written appraisal for each parcel or separate piece of real estate should be obtained. In most cases this can be done by a local real estate broker or agent.

In community property states, only the decedent's one-half of each asset is counted. A couple would have to own assets of more than $3,000,000 before an estate tax would be due. (The decedent's one-half would need to be over $1,500,000 if he or she died in 2004.)

The new valuation also establishes the value for income tax purposes if the asset is later sold. If the decedent purchased his or her home years ago for $100,000, but it is worth $400,000 at death, the people who inherit the home will only pay income tax if they later sell the home for more than $400,000.

Valuing assets is one of the things which you will need to have an attorney, accountant, or other financial planner help you with. Before you see such a professional, you should make a list of all real estate, securities, bank accounts, employee benefits, life insurance, tangible personal property, or other assets which the decedent owned at the time of death.

CASUALTY INSURANCE FOR ASSETS

One important consideration is to verify insurance on the decedent's assets. Few things are worse than when the decedent's home burns down shortly after his or her death and you discover that it is underinsured, or worse yet, not insured at all.

You, or the executor or trustee should immediately check into insurance coverage. You should purchase insurance to include coverage of the home and contents and any automobiles, boats, or other important assets. Insurance should be verified both for the replacement value (how much you receive if the asset is destroyed) and also the amount of liability coverage. The mailing address for premiums and other correspondence should be changed to that of the executor or other person who inherits so that future notices and insurance premium notices go to the correct party.

Many people maintain insurance but have underinsured their assets. A house may have been insured for $100,000 twenty years ago. However, if the value of the house is $400,000 today, the $100,000 coverage is not adequate. The same may be true for the liability coverage. Whoever is responsible for the decedent's assets should discuss the coverage with the insurance company or agent handling the policy shortly after death. Whoever is inheriting the property should be named as an "additional insured" on the policy. If the asset is in probate, the estate should be named, until the estate assets are distributed.

Some insurance companies refuse to raise the limits of coverage after a person dies. A few insurance companies refuse to renew the insurance after death. You, as the executor, trustee, or person inheriting the assets, should immediately check with your insurance agent or company regarding coverage if there is any difficulty in keeping the insurance on the asset. In any event, you should contact the insurance company which had the coverage on the policy or the agent who wrote the policy immediately after the decedent's death.

If coverage is canceled or the company refuses to renew the policy, the executor or person handling the assets should check with his or her own personal insurance company to see if coverage can be obtained or a rider put on that person's policy to temporarily provide coverage until the legal matters are concluded and assets are distributed. Some assets, such as vehicles, boats and furniture, may be distributed or sold shortly after death to reduce the liability and the need for insurance coverage.

•   PLAN AHEAD

It is very common for people to underinsure their homes. Real estate prices have climbed extraordinarily over the last 25 years. Some people update their insurance on a regular basis to reflect this, but many don't. Since the chances of your house burning down right after your death are relatively low, you might feel that this is an acceptable risk. Nevertheless, this sort of thing has happened, and it would probably be a serious financial setback for your loved ones if it did. Review your insurance coverage with the agent (who is listed on the policy) or the insurance company.

Keep an itemized list of your insurance policies which lists the insurance company and its address, assets covered, policy number, and amount of coverage. If there is an insurance agent or broker, be sure to list his or her name, address, and telephone number.

SAFE DEPOSIT BOX

In many states, safe deposit boxes are no longer sealed at death and inventoried by a government agency. However, in other states, safe deposit boxes are still sealed and inventoried.

If the safe deposit box has another signer on the box, the other signer or signers may legally enter the box and remove anything they wish. If there is no co-signer on the box, then generally anyone who has a certified copy of the death certificate and the key to the box may enter the box to search for and remove the decedent's will and any burial instructions. A representative of the financial institution will accompany the person to be sure nothing else is removed.

If there is no co-signer and there are no probate proceedings, then the people who inherit the decedent's assets can usually fill out a form after the decedent's death, enter the safe deposit box, and remove the contents.

If there is a probate, the executor or administrator may legally enter the box after being appointed by the court and remove all of the contents.

If the box is sealed, you should make an appointment with the state agency to inventory the contents of the box. (It may take several weeks to schedule the appointment.) Obviously, you will need the keys to the box to enter it. If the key has been lost and can't be found, the financial institution will generally have it drilled open. The institution will probably charge a significant fee for this. If there are co-signers on the box, they can enter it after it is inventoried. Otherwise, the executor or administrator will have to do this. If someone has a power of attorney for the decedent, the power of attorney terminated at the time of the person's death and the agent (the person with the power of attorney) cannot enter the box.

• **PLAN AHEAD**

Talk to someone at the institution where you keep your safe deposit box and find out what will happen to it after your death. Will the box be inventoried? If so, what government agency inventories it and who should be contacted? How long does it take to get an appointment? In addition to all of this, it is a good idea to keep a list of what you keep in the safe deposit box. It can be very disconcerting trying to find documents or items after someone's death and not knowing whether they are in the decedent's safe deposit box or not. Let your loved ones know what you keep in the box and the easiest way they can get access to it after your death. Be sure that they know where the key to the box is located.

It is also a good idea to have another family member as a co-signer on the box, or for a husband and wife, to have a third party as a co-signer. That way, after your death someone can enter the box without waiting for an executor or administrator to be appointed.

MEDICAL INSURANCE

If the decedent was receiving Medicaid benefits from the state, the state must be notified then after the death. If there is an executor or administrator, then he or she must give notice to the proper state authorities. If there is no probate, then the people who inherit the decedent's assets should give this notice within a period of time of the date of death. This period varies from state to state.

The purpose of this notification is to allow the state to seek reimbursement for all benefits paid for the decedent prior to death. The state can file a creditor's claim in the decedent's estate, if there is one, or demand and sue for the value of all benefits previously paid by the state from the people who inherit if there is no probate proceeding.

Don't confuse Medicaid with Medicare. Medicare is a government financed program for health insurance and does not seek reimbursement. Medicaid is a federal and state government program to finance medical costs for those who are unable to pay them. If a Medicaid participant dies and it is discovered that he or she does own enough assets to cover past medical costs, then Medicaid requires repayment.

If the decedent had unpaid medical bills at the time of his or her death (and most people do) then someone has to file the required medical claim forms. Usually these are first filed with the local Medicare processing agent if the person was covered by Medicare. After payment is made, a claim is then filed with any supplemental insurance carrier.

If the decedent was not covered by Medicare (if he or she was under age 65) medical claim forms should be filed directly with the insurance company. If there are any questions, you should phone the insurance company to verify the procedure and to obtain the current claim forms.

Most insurance carriers want additional information about who is filing the forms, and if there is reimbursement for benefits already paid by the decedent, who receives the benefits. If there is a probate, the benefits will normally go to the estate. If there is no probate, benefits are usually paid to the nearest relatives or others who are entitled to them.

If there is a surviving spouse or children covered by the policy, you should contact the company personnel office (for a group plan) or the insurance company regarding continuing medical coverage for the survivor or survivors.

• **PLAN AHEAD**

Dealing with medical bills and claims is one of the major difficulties and sources of frustration for survivors when someone dies. Make sure that your loved ones know the name of your medical insurance, the policy number, and whom to contact regarding questions.

Many doctors and hospitals take an assignment of benefits. This means that they collect the benefits and then bill the estate or relatives for the balance.

There are a few commercial firms which handle all of the paperwork and submit the claims for an annual fee. If you have a large number of medical bills and it looks as if it will be time consuming dealing with all of them, you might want to consider such a firm. Check the yellow pages or your local hospital or medical association for the names of such firms.

Done 7-21-08

SOCIAL SECURITY

Any social security payments which the decedent might have been receiving stop after the date of death. For this reason, you should notify the local social security office shortly after the date of death. Usually, a telephone call to the local social security office is sufficient.

The social security administration makes payment during a month for the prior month. A check issued on November 3rd is for social security benefits for the month of October. If the decedent died during October, the funds are not prorated. A person must live through midnight on the last day of the month to be entitled to payment. If John Doe dies on October 30th, the payment made on November 3rd for the month of October must be returned.

If a check is issued for social security benefits, the check should be returned, unopened with the notation "deceased" and the date of death written across the front of the envelope. If a direct deposit is made to a bank or savings and loan account, the funds should be left on deposit, since they will be reclaimed by the social security administration within approximately 60 days.

It takes the social security administration approximately 15 days to stop payments. If they are notified by the 15th of the month, they can normally stop the check issued on the third of the following month.

If there is a surviving spouse, minor children, or incapacitated adult children, a $255 death benefit is payable if the decedent had paid into the social security system. Minor children or adult incapacitated children may continue to receive payments for a period of time depending on the circumstances. If none of these relatives survives, no death benefit is payable.

If there is a surviving spouse, the spouse is normally entitled to 100% of the decedent's social security payments or the amount he or she would draw under social security, whichever is higher. Benefits are only payable to the surviving spouse if he or she has attained 62 years of age or older (for reduced benefits) or 65 years of age (for full benefits).

If the decedent was receiving social security benefits, you should phone the local social security office within a few days of the death. Most social security offices prefer to handle the initial contact by phone rather than in person. The only information they will want will be the decedent's name, date of death, and social security number. If there are any payable death benefits or benefits payable to a spouse or others, the social security office can advise you regarding what to do. If social security was handled by direct deposit to a financial institution, that institution should also be notified that the deposit can be returned if made after death.

Many funeral homes and mortuaries contact social security and give them the information regarding the decedent. However, many times the funeral home or mortuary states that they will take care of this but in reality neglect to do so. You should probably contact the social security office yourself to make sure that they are informed of the decedent's death.

• **PLAN AHEAD**

You should determine what documents will be needed at death for your spouse to receive social security. You should also know approximately how much will be paid to your spouse. The local social security office can give you this information.

RETIREMENT AND ANNUITY BENEFITS

There are two major concerns regarding retirement and annuity benefits. First, are there any further benefits payable after the decedent's death? Second, if there are payable benefits, is a beneficiary designation required and who is the beneficiary?

If the decedent was receiving a monthly pension or annuity payment, the payment checks dated after the date of death should not be cashed. If a check is dated prior to the date of death or on the date of death itself, it can still be cashed. If it is dated after the date of death, it should be returned to the issuing organization along with a certified copy of the death certificate and a letter asking if any further payments will be made.

Some companies prorate the monthly payment so that if a person dies in the middle of the month, half of the monthly payment is made. However, many companies do not prorate the monthly amount.

In some cases further benefits are payable to the surviving spouse, to minor children, or to other designated beneficiaries. All of this depends upon the terms of the pension or annuity. If it is a joint and survivor pension, a surviving spouse will receive some monthly amount for his or her lifetime. If the decedent contributed to a plan (such as a government retirement plan) and died before receiving all of his or her contribution, the balance of the contribution will be paid to the named beneficiary.

Each plan or annuity varies, so it is important to contact the trustees of the pension plan, the personnel department of the company the decedent retired from or whoever is responsible for the administration of the plan. In some cases this is an insurance or annuity company.

Sometimes people purchase a single premium annuity policy, which is more of an investment than an annuity policy. Suppose someone buys a single premium annuity policy, placing $100,000 with the annuity company. The earnings on the policy accumulate income tax-free. The person dies before taking any money out of the policy. The policy is worth $150,000 at the time of the person's death. The policy has a named beneficiary who receives the funds. Unfortunately, the $50,000 increase in value is taxable as ordinary income when it is withdrawn by the beneficiary. If you are the beneficiary of such an account, you shouldn't take the payment without first reviewing all possible payment and tax options with the annuity company or with an accountant. In many cases the beneficiary can elect to receive payments over a period of time.

• PLAN AHEAD

Keep records regarding any pension retirement and annuity policies or accounts. Each record should indicate what is payable, if anything, after your death. Make sure that whoever is listed as the designated beneficiary knows that he or she is the beneficiary and knows whom to contact after your death.

CREDIT CARDS, UNPAID SALARY, AND UNCASHED TRAVELERS CHECKS

Most people have credit cards in their name when they die. If they are not retired, there is often unpaid salary and possibly vacation and sick leave which is payable after death. And a surprising number of people die with uncashed travelers checks.

CREDIT CARDS

When a person dies, the credit cards in his or her name should be canceled. The executor or person handling the decedent's assets should cut up each credit card and mail the cut card by certified mail to the issuing financial institution with a letter indicating that the person has died and that the account should be closed. The institution should be instructed as to where to send any outstanding bill.

If the account was in the name of the husband but other parties such as the wife or a child had cards, these cards will also be canceled because of the death of the only account holder. If the spouse, children, or others want to have these cards reissued, then it is normally necessary to make a separate application with the organization which issued the card.

UNPAID SALARY

If the decedent was employed at the time of death, there may be unpaid salary, vacation benefits, or other benefits. Frequently, state law allows up to a certain dollar amount to be paid immediately to the surviving spouse, if there is one, without probate. If there is no surviving spouse, the benefits will be paid to the decedent's estate if there is a probate, or to the people who inherit if there is no probate.

The company personnel office should be contacted to determine what benefits are payable and to obtain the necessary forms to get the benefits.

UNCASHED TRAVELERS CHECKS

While travelers checks are used somewhat less than they were in the days before ATM machines and easy credit card access around the world, people still often have uncashed traveler's checks at the time of death. If an administrator or executor is appointed to handle the estate, a certified copy of the documents appointing the person will be needed to cash in the checks.

If there are no probate proceedings, the relative or relatives who are entitled to the funds can usually fill out a declaration after the date of death and collect the funds directly without probate.

The organization which issued the traveler's checks such as American Express, VISA, etc. should be contacted to obtain the required forms and information on where to submit the uncashed checks.

FREQUENT FLIER MILES

Many people have accumulated mileage or points under airline and other plans, such as American Express, Hilton Hotels, etc. The transfer of the points on miles varies with each organization. Some allow transfer to anyone, and many allow tranfer to immediate family members, but a few allow no transfer, with the rewards expiring at death.

Each organization should be contacted to advise of the death and to obtain information about policy on the transfer of miles or points.

• PLAN AHEAD

Make sure that your loved ones know where you keep your credit cards (if not in your wallet). They should also have the addresses to which they can send the cut up credit cards, the address, phone number, and contact person in your company's personnel office, and a phone number or address to contact regarding any traveler's checks.

LUMP SUM PENSION, PROFIT SHARING, IRA
AND OTHER BENEFITS

In many cases the decedent was covered by an IRA account, corporate profit sharing or lump sum pension plan, self-employed retirement plan (Keogh plan) or other type of benefit. If the decedent was covered by such a plan, the benefits in the plan are payable to the named beneficiary. If there is no named or living beneficiary, then the benefits are normally payable to the decedent's estate and pass by the will or by intestate succession.

It is not unusual for someone who has retired and rolled a large lump sum retirement benefit over to a rollover IRA account to divide up the account among a number of bank accounts, brokerage firm accounts, and mutual funds. Someone with a $1,000,000 rollover may have from one to fifteen separate IRA accounts.

The taxability of the benefits at death is very complex. The benefits are taxable for federal estate tax purposes based on the total "fair market value" of all of the accounts. If the benefits are paid to the surviving spouse and the spouse is a United States citizen, the benefits are not taxable for estate tax purposes.

Secondly, the benefits are normally taxable for income tax purposes (as ordinary income and not as capital gains) when the benefits are paid from the plan. If the surviving spouse is the beneficiary, the spouse, but only the spouse, may roll over the benefits to a new IRA account in his or her name, tax-free. The new IRA is then considered the spouse's IRA. If someone other than the spouse is the beneficiary, then the benefits must be withdrawn over a maximum period of time, which varies greatly depending on many factors.

The Internal Revenue Service has issued extensive regulations to supplement the Internal Revenue Code regarding how rapidly benefits must be withdrawn after someone's death. The period varies depending on the age of the decedent, the age of the beneficiary or

beneficiaries, and whether the beneficiary is the spouse of the decedent. If there are no designated beneficiaries, or all named beneficiaries are deceased, the IRA benefits will be paid to the participant's
estate and pass by his or her will. This may involve probate.

Many IRA plans have less flexible methods of distribution. One
major brokerage firm formerly had an IRA plan that provided that
all benefits be payable within two years of the date of death even
though federal laws allowed a longer period. Such provisions govern
the assets in their plan.

Before a beneficiary draws out any benefits, he or she should consult the plan administrator, an accountant, or attorney regarding the
available options for withdrawal and the tax ramifications of each
option.

• PLAN AHEAD

Usually when you open an IRA account, you are given a large
folder with a copy of the plan, designation forms, and other documents. Keep all of these, and let your loved ones know where they
are. Keep all of them neatly in separate folders. Secondly, keep the
beneficiary designations up-to-date. Any benefits payable after death
are paid to a named beneficiary. Most corporate plans require that
the spouse be named as the beneficiary. However, some plans allow
you to name others or change the beneficiary designation. Make sure
your records reflect any changes that you make.

WORKERS' COMPENSATION BENEFITS

If the decedent was killed during the course of employment and it is a "work related" death, benefits might be payable. In most states these benefits are limited to a spouse, minor children and, in some cases, other dependent relatives.

If the decedent was disabled and receiving benefits, the benefits normally terminate at death. If, however, the death was related to the disability a lump sum benefit may be payable to certain relatives. This lump sum varies from state to state, but can go as high as $150,000 in some states. This is frequently referred to as "workers'" or "workman's" compensation.

If there is any question as to whether the decedent was eligible for benefits, an attorney who specializes in worker's or workmen's compensation should be contacted. Workers' compensation is generally handled by non-court proceedings under a state administered procedure.

The procedure is rather complicated and an attorney, who is a specialist in this filed, should be consulted. Normally, the attorney receives a percentage of the benefits which are received, and this amount is set by state law. Workers' compensation benefits may be handled through a state administered fund or by a private insurance company. A few large companies are allowed to "self-insure," without using a fund or insurance company.

If the state Workmen's Compensation Fund pays out benefits and a lawsuit is later brought by a third party to obtain money for the disability or death, the fund has the right to seek reimbursement for the funds paid from such a lawsuit or settlement.

John Doe dies at work due to defective machinery. The workers' insurance fund pays $100,000 to his spouse. The widow later sues the machinery manufacturer and receives $1,000,000. The workers' fund has the right to be reimbursed for their $100,000 death benefit from the $1,000,000 which the widow received.

States vary significantly in how they treat work-related deaths. In some states, if the death was caused by stress of emotional difficulty due to job related problems, or even in some cases of suicide, benefits may be payable. In other states, stress, emotional problems and the like won't even be considered as a basis for workers' compensation.

If there is any question as to whether the death was work related or not (such as a question of whether possible asbestos exposure might have caused lung cancer, etc.), an attorney who specializes in workers' compensation should be contacted soon after death. There are statutes of limitations regarding how long the relatives have to bring an action. If someone waits too long, he or she may not be able to bring an action.

LIFE INSURANCE

A large number, perhaps a majority, of people have some sort of life insurance coverage when they die. The policy may be a paid company policy in existence since retirement or a small policy of $1,000 which was purchased 40 to 50 years ago. While the life insurance benefits are the primary concern when someone dies, the decedent might have also had credit life insurance and accidental death benefits.

LIFE INSURANCE BENEFITS

Life insurance proceeds are payable to the named beneficiary and not to the decedent's estate. If there is no designated beneficiary or if all of the named beneficiaries have died before the decedent, then the benefits are payable to the estate. If the decedent was covered by a government retirement plan such as State Teacher's Retirement, Public Employees Retirement or another similar plan, there may be a death benefit payable, which is treated the same as life insurance.

The beneficiary should contact the insurance company or plan administrator to obtain the necessary claim form. The only requirements to obtain the benefits are generally a life insurance company claim form, certified copy of the death certificate, and, sometimes, the policy itself. If the policy was a group policy, such as those issued by an employer or professional association, the beneficiary should contact the employer or organization.

Life insurance proceeds are not taxable for income tax purposes. Interest on the funds paid by the insurance company after death is taxable for income tax purposes. Insurance proceeds are generally taxable for federal estate tax purposes unless someone other than the decedent owned the policy.

CREDIT LIFE INSURANCE

Many people purchase credit life insurance to cover loans and to have the loans paid at death. So-called credit life insurance may be purchased to cover a home loan, car loan, credit card charges, or other debts. Sometimes the insurance is arranged at the time of purchase through the credit agency involved. Other times it is purchased separately.

At death the creditor may not know of the existence of a credit life policy or may forget that the decedent took out credit life insurance. If the decedent owed any debts at death, particularly large debts such as a home loan or automobile loan, the creditor should be requested to check to see if any separate credit life insurance policy existed.

ACCIDENTAL DEATH BENEFITS

Many people purchase accidental death benefits. These are basically life insurance policies which pay out only if the person dies from accidental causes, such as an automobile accident or in an airplane crash. Accidental life insurance may be part of a travel package or purchase, included when an airfare is charged with an American Express card, for instance, or it may be a small amount of coverage, such as an accidental death benefit with auto association coverage.

If a person dies accidentally, the relatives should check to see if there is any coverage for accidental death benefits. Even existing policies may have double indemnity (twice the face amount) if the person died accidentally. Automobile insurance polices and even automobile club membership may cover some death benefits.

Years ago I handled an estate for a woman killed in Burma on a local airline. She had purchased her tickets using her American Express card and obtained supplemental accidental insurance in the amount of $150,000. However, after investigation, it was determined that the only portion of the trip not paid for in advance was the Burma flight, which was paid for in cash locally. The insurance failed to cover her because this portion of the trip was not charged on her credit card. No insurance was payable.

• **PLAN AHEAD**

It is very important to know who the beneficiary of your life insurance policy is. You are required to fill out a beneficiary designation when you take out life insurance. You can change the beneficiary designation by filling out a separate form. Keep copies of these forms and let your loved ones know where they are. If you can't find the forms and are unsure whom you have designated as the beneficiary, contact the insurance company or the organization that handles group policies.

In most cases a husband and wife will designate each other as beneficiaries. Generally, secondary beneficiaries are named so that if the husband and wife are killed together, as in a car accident, the insurance proceeds will pass without probate to others, such as to the children. Make sure your secondary beneficiaries know who they are.

Some policies, such as accidental death benefits from credit card firms, automobile associations and others do not normally have beneficiary forms. The benefits are frequently payable to the estate and go through probate. In some cases, a beneficiary form can be obtained, but the organization must be contacted and such a form specifically requested.

TAX CONCERNS

The old saying that nothing is certain except death and taxes is truer than most people realize. Federal estate taxes, state inheritance taxes, federal and state income taxes, and other taxes may all be due because of someone's death.

It is important to have the decedent's income tax returns for the three years prior to death. The executor or nearest relative who is handling the decedent's financial matters should verify that he or she has the returns for the last three years. If the returns cannot be found, then the accountant or tax preparer, if any, who handled the returns should be asked to provide copies.

If returns cannot be located, the Internal Revenue Service and the state tax authority can be contacted to obtain copies of returns. A specific form is filled out and a fee paid. Generally, the returns can be obtained for the last three years.

It is also important to obtain copies of any federal gift tax returns filed by the decedent at any time, copies of any estate tax return for any predeceased spouse, and copies of all trust income tax returns if the decedent was the beneficiary or the trustee of any trust at the time of death.

If you have experience preparing and filing tax returns and the decedent's financial affairs were not too complicated, you might be able to do the returns yourself. But in most cases, it will be wiser (and cheaper in the long run) to go to an accountant or professional tax preparer. If the decedent had an accountant or tax preparer, you should contact him or her. If you feel comfortable with this person, it will probably be easier to let him or her prepare any necessary tax returns than to find someone else to do them. However, if you don't feel comfortable with the decedent's accountant or tax preparer, you can always get someone else to do the returns.

What sorts of returns need to be filed? Unless the decedent was in a very low income category, he or she has had to file an income tax return every year. A return must still be filed for the year in which the decedent dies.

Has the decedent given away more than $11,000 in cash or assets to any one person during the calendar year? If so, a gift tax return must be filed although there will be no tax on the gift unless the decedent gave away more than $1,000,000 in addition to the $11,000 annual gift. The gift tax exemption increased on January 1, 2002, from $10,000/year per donee to $11,000/year per donee.

If the decedent owned more than the estate tax exemption, $1,500,000 to3,500,000, depending on the year of death, a federal estate tax return must be filed within nine months of the date of death. This is true even if no tax is due. However, the IRS will grant an extension of up to six months to file the return if necessary. In addition to the federal estate tax, many states have their own estate taxes. Some states have inheritance taxes (which are calculated differently than estate taxes.)

By their nature, taxes are complicated. Even more so than for the other concerns covered in this book, you should remember that the following information regarding tax concerns is only the most bare-bone summary. There are, quite literally, libraries of books, journals, digests, and CD-ROM's of information on tax issues, much of which is applicable when somebody dies. As a generalization, the more money a person had, the more complicated the tax situation will be when he or she dies. But this isn't always the case. Many wealthy people plan their estates and taxes very carefully so that their estates pass to their beneficiaries relatively smoothly with the minimum possible taxes paid. Conversely, many times the decedent is relatively poor, but has neglected to pay taxes or even file a return for years. In such situations, what little money there is in the estate often goes toward sorting out the tax problems. Whatever the situation you face, you will almost always be better off reviewing the situation with an accountant or other professional tax preparer. The following information should give you a rough idea of the issues involved and questions to ask.

FINAL INCOME TAX RETURNS

When a person dies, income tax returns must still be filed. Death does not excuse tax returns or the payment of taxes.

If the decedent died early in the year and the prior year's tax returns were still due, they must be filed. Suppose John Doe dies on February 3rd. The return for the prior year needs to be filed by April 15th. Many people obtain extensions to file their tax returns. Income tax extensions can run as late as October 15th for the prior year. If a person dies with a prior year's return due, the surviving spouse, executor or other relative will still have to file the return. If an extension is needed it can be obtained, but not beyond October 15th.

An income tax return must also be filed for the period from January 1st through the date of death. If Frank Doe dies on September 29th, a return will be required for that year, but will only cover the period January 1st–September 29th. This return is due by April 15th of the following year.

Income which comes in after September 29th and deductions paid after that date will not be reported on the decedent's final income tax return. They will be picked up on an estate, trust, or surviving joint tenants return, depending on the situation at death.

Income from January 1st until the date of death is picked up on this return. Income which comes in after the date of death will be picked up on the estate income tax return or on a trust return or on the return of a joint tenant, if the asset was in joint tenancy. Deductions such as mortgage interest and taxes can only be taken off if paid prior to death. The only exception is medical expenses. If they are paid within one year of death they can be deducted on the final income tax return.

Exemptions, standard deductions, and tax rates are not prorated for the year of death. For tax computation purposes, the decedent is treated as if he or she was alive for the entire year.

If there is a surviving spouse, a joint income tax return may be filed for the year of death. If there is no spouse, the return must be signed by the executor or administrator of the decedent's estate. If there is no probate, then whoever has the assets or handles the estate is responsible for filing the return.

The return should contain the address to which the IRS will mail any future refund or notices. The top of the tax return should be labeled "Deceased" followed by the date of death.

The Internal Revenue Service has the right to audit a tax return for up to three years after it is filed. Many state tax authorities can audit up to four years after filing. If there is a tax deficiency on audit, then whoever has inherited the assets, such as the surviving spouse, executor or administrator, or other relatives is legally responsible for paying the tax due.

After someone dies, the accountant or tax preparer should be contacted to prepare the final income tax returns and review any estimated tax payments for the year of death to see if these estimated tax payments should be made. If a balance is due, the balance needs to be paid with the return. Any estimated income tax payments need to be taken into account so that full credit is received. If a refund is due, IRS form 1310 should be completed and attached to the return. If a refund is payable, it will be paid

1) To the surviving spouse if it is a joint return;

2) To the executor or administrator if there is a probate;

3) To the person legally entitled to the refund if there is no probate.

• PLAN AHEAD

Proper accounting and income tax preparation are beyond the scope of this book. Suffice it to say, that you should keep your tax and financial information in good order and that your family should know who has prepared your taxes for the last few years.

GIFT TAX RETURNS

It is possible that a gift tax return was due when the decedent died. A gift tax return is due if the decedent gave over $11,000 in cash or assets to any one person during a calendar year. The return is normally due on April 15th of the year following the year of gift, or, if a person dies, within nine months of the date of death, if this is earlier than the following April 15th.

If a person gives $15,000 to his son on October 20th and then dies a few days later, the return is due by the following April 15th. If the person gives $15,000 to his son on February 10th and then dies on March 16th, the return is due nine months from the date of death, or by December 16th of that year.

In most cases no tax is payable, and the gift tax return is only an information return. The federal government's unified exemption, over and above the $11,000 per year per person exemption, is $1,500,000 to 3,500,000, depending on the year of death. Unless you give away more than the $1,000,000(the gift tax exemption does not increase in future years) in addition to the $11,000, no tax will be due. At death, all gifts of over $10,000 or $11,000 per year are added back to the decedent's estate for estate tax purposes. If Frank Doe gives his son $111,000 this year, he will need to file a gift tax return but no tax will be due. When he dies, $100,000 of this gift is added to whatever assets he owns at death.

All gift tax returns must be prepared before it is possible to prepare the federal estate tax return. If there is an accountant or tax preparer, he or she will do the return. The federal gift tax return is Internal Revenue Service form 709. Some states also have their own gift taxes. If a federal return is required, you should contact your state tax authority to see if a state return is also due. If a state return is due, the due date is generally the same date as that of the federal return. If a gift of over $11,000 has been made and a gift tax return has not been filed, this should be discussed with the attorney or accountant.

If a gift of over $10,000 or $11,000 per year was previously made (depending upon the year of the gift) but a gift tax return was not filed, this also should be discussed with the attorney or accountant.

The executor or person handling the decedent's assets should also determine if any prior gift tax returns have been filed. These will be needed.

• **PLAN AHEAD**

You should keep copies of all federal and state gift tax returns which you have ever filed. These returns will be needed after you die when someone prepares and files a federal estate tax return. The federal estate tax and federal gift tax are combined under a unified tax structure. When someone dies, all of the prior taxable gifts (over $10,000 or $11,000 per year per person) since approximately 1977 are added back to the decedent's assets.

The federal government keeps track of these returns and if they are not listed on the estate tax return, the IRS will usually spin its computers and advise the person administering the estate that he or she has omitted these figures.

FEDERAL ESTATE TAX RETURN

One very important concern, which needs to be resolved within four to eight weeks after the death, is whether a federal estate tax return must be filed or not. The United States government has a death tax system known as the United States Estate Tax. If the decedent was a U.S. citizen or a permanent U.S. resident and if he or she owned more than $1,500,000 to 3,500,000 of assets, depending on the year of death, (disregarding liabilities,) a return is due. If a return is due, it must be filed within nine months of the date of death, even if no tax is due. However, an extension of up to six months can be obtained, if needed.

All of the decedents assets, even those located in foreign countries, are counted for federal estate tax purposes. Stocks, bank accounts, life insurance, mutual funds, retirement benefits, IRA accounts, and all other types of assets are included. If there is a tax due, all of the assets can be valued at the fair market value as of either the date of death or six months after the date of death. The lower value can be used.

After the assets are valued, various deductions and exemptions can be applied. All debts which the decedent owed at the time of death are deductible. These would include unpaid bills, a home mortgage, and bank loans. Also, expenses related to the death itself are deductible. These might include funeral and burial costs, legal fees, probate costs, and accountant's fees.

Any amount left to a "qualified" charity can also be deducted. A qualified charity is one which has an exemption letter from the IRS. The decedent's beneficiaries cannot make a gift to a charity with the decedent's money; the gift must pass by the decedent's will, trust, beneficiary designation, or some other such method. There is no limit on the amount which someone can leave to a charity or charities at the time of his or her death. Some people leave everything they own to a charity or charities.

A person can also leave any amount to his or her spouse tax-free, provided that the surviving spouse is a U.S. citizen. Usually, when the first spouse dies and all or most of the assets are left to the surviving spouse, no tax is due.

If the decedent died with over $1,500,000 to 3,500,000 of assets, and if after deducting the debts, charitable gifts, and the amount left to the surviving spouse, the net value of the estate is still over this exempt amount, federal estate tax will be due. The excess over the exemption is taxed at a rate of between 45% and 48%. The exemption, tax due and tax rates are on page 108.

If a return is not filed within nine months of the date of death, a tax is due, and if an extension has not been requested, there are penalties and interest on the amount due. The federal estate tax return (IRS form 706) is complex. It should be done by a professional. Don't attempt to do it yourself.

If the decedent's estate does not have enough cash to pay the estate tax, it may obtain an extension to pay the taxes for up to ten years. In such situations the tax must be paid in installments, and the IRS charges interest at its current rate. If the estate includes real estate and an estate tax is due and deferred, the IRS can place a lien on the property. If the property is sold before the deferred tax is paid, the IRS can then collect any tax due from proceeds of the sale.

Once the estate tax return has been filed, the IRS has three years from either the due date or filing date (whichever is later) to audit the estate and assess any deficiency in payments. In reality, the IRS will usually make a decision whether or not to audit the estate within eight to twelve months after the estate tax return is filed. If the IRS decides not to audit the estate, it will issue an "estate tax closing letter" and send it to the person administering the estate. If the IRS decides to audit the estate it will send a personal letter requesting additional information. Audits generally occur when there is a question regarding the following: 1) value of assets, especially real property and business interests, 2) deductions on the return, 3) transfer of assets before the decedent's death. If the IRS assesses a deficiency and demands more tax, the person administering the estate can appeal this in a tax court.

Assets which are subject to the federal estate tax get a new cost basis for income tax. This means that in computing capital gains or losses the new figure (the value at the time of the decedent's death or six months later) is used as the cost basis. This works to the advantage of whoever inherits the asset. Many people own real property, stocks, or other assets that have increased dramatically in value over the years. If these assets were sold, the capital gains tax would be based on the old (lower) price.

- **PLAN AHEAD**

As with many other concerns discussed in this book, having an itemized list of your assets will make the job of valuing your assets and determining whether a federal estate tax return must be filed much easier. In addition, while estate planning may not entirely eliminate federal estate taxes, it is the rare estate where some tax saving cannot be accomplished by careful planning. Consulting an estate planning attorney now will probably result in significant tax savings for your loved ones after your death.

UNITED STATES FEDERAL ESTATE TAX RATES

In 1997, Congress increased the federal estate tax exemption from a maximum of $600,000 to $1,000,000, to be phased in from 1997 to 2002.

In early 2001, Congress increased the estate tax exemption from $1,000,000 to 3,500,000, to be phased in from 2002 to 2009. Congress then abolished the estate tax effective 2010. However, they also put in a "sunset provision" whereby Congress had to confirm this law prior to 2011, or the estate tax would come back January 1, 2011, with the exemption and rates in effect in 2002. Congress will likely make more changes in the estate tax law prior to 2010.

The exemption and rates in effect from 2004 through 2009 are as follows:

Year	Exemption	Tax Rates OverExemption
2004	1,500,000	45-48
2005	1,500,000	45-47
2006	2,000,000	46
2007	2,000,000	45
2008	2,000,000	45
2009	3,500,000	45

The amount of estate tax due, including the above exemption, for various estate is as follows:

Amount of Estate Tax Due

Total Estate	2004	2005	2006	2007	2008	2009
$ 1,500,000	0	0	0	0	0	0
2,000,000	225,000	225,000	0	0	0	0
2,500,000	465,000	450,000	230,000	225,000	225,000	0
3,000,000	705,000	695,000	460,000	450,000	450,000	0
3,500,000	945,000	925,000	690,000	675,000	675,000	0
Rate-excess	48%	47%	46%	45%	45%	45%

GENERATION -SKIPPING TRANSFER TAX

While the federal estate tax is complicated, many people are amazed to learn that there is also a second death tax, which is imposed in some estates. This is an additional tax, which is paid after the estate tax is determined.

This tax, which was imposed starting in the late 1980s, was designed to prevent people from setting up trusts for their descendants and having the assets in trust for 50-100 years with no estate taxes paid during that period. John Doe dies and an estate tax is due at this death. He leaves his assests to his son, James Doe, and when the son dies, the estate tax is imposed on the son's assets. If John Doe left assets in trust for James, then when James died there would be no estate tax due.

The above is still the rule but to prevent the escape of the second tax when the son dies, the federal government imposes a generation-skippping transfer tax. This tax is imposed if the person's assets pass to a generation below that of his or her children, such as greandchildren, great grandchildren, etc. It also applies when assets are left in trust, as described above, and ultimately go to the second or younger generation without estate tax.

The tax applies not only to direct gifts or bequests to grandchildren and others, but to certain irrevocable trusts that ultimately go to these people if the trust was irrevocable after October 22, 1986.

The exemption from this generation-skipping transfer tax is the same exemption as the estate tax, $1,500,000 to $3,500,000 with the tax rate on the excess being the highest estate tax rate then in force, 45-48%, as follows.

Year	Exemption	Tax Rate
2004	1,500,000	48%
2005	1,500,000	47%
2006	2,000,000	46%
2007	2,000,000	45%
2008	2,000,000	45%
2009	3,500,000	45%

This tax is rather complicated with various rules depending upon whether the assets go directly to granchildren or others or later comes out of an irrevocable trust to grandchildren or others.

If you think the amount going to a "skipped" generation is more than the exemption, then you may wish to discuss this with your accountant or attorney.

STATE INHERITANCE AND ESTATE TAX RETURNS

Some states have a death tax structure known as an inheritance tax. An estate tax, which the United States uses, is based on the total assets owned by the decedent. It does not matter if the assets are left to three children, eight grandchildren, or 42 nieces and nephews. The tax is based on the decedent's assets. A few states have a similar estate tax structure.

An inheritance tax, on the other hand, is based on the relationship of each person who inherits assets. The tax is composed of a number of sub-tax totals, one for each person who inherits the assets. A separate exemption and tax rate may exist for each child, brother and sister, cousin or person not related to the decedent. The state in which the decedent resided determines the tax. If the decedent left $300,000 equally to his three children, then each child would receive $100,000. If the inheritance tax exempts $50,000 per child and taxes the excess at 3%, then each child would owe an inheritance tax of $1,500. ($100,000-$50,000 = $50,000. 3% of $50,000 = $1,500.)

Most states do **not** have a separate inheritance tax or estate tax structure. At the time of the writing of this book, the following states have a separate inheritance or estate tax structure:

Connecticut
Indiana
Iowa
Kentucky
Nebraska
New Hampshire
New Jersey
Ohio (estate tax)
Oklahoma (estate tax)
Pennsylvania
Tennessee

In the past, a portion of the federal estate tax has passed to the state in which the decedent resided or owned real property. This has been under a rather complicated formula that ranged from 3-10% of the estate value. This "state death tax credit" is being phased out, and starting in 2006 it will be eliminated. As a result many states which did not have a "death tax" are now imposing an estate or inheritance tax.

In many states which have an inheritance or estate tax, assets cannot be transferred without obtaining a tax release from local tax authorities. Safe deposit boxes may or may not be inventoried by the state after death.

• PLAN AHEAD

Ask your accountant or tax preparer if your state has a separate inheritance or estate tax structure. If it does, find out what information may be needed after death. Obtain copies of the appropriate state forms.

Also determine if safe deposit boxes are sealed after death and the contents cannot be removed until the box is inventoried, or if tax releases are required to release bank accounts and other assets.

PLANNING AHEAD: A ROUGH GUIDE

True planning ahead for your death involves estate planning, which falls outside the scope of this book. Different states have different laws and tax structures, so estate planning is somewhat different in each state. Most people want to minimize the costs, hassles and taxes involved when someone dies. To do that, and to do it correctly, you should consult with an attorney who specializes in estate planning. Many people are hesitant about attorneys' fees and, if at all possible, will avoid seeing an attorney. After all, if you can get a pre-printed will or trust out of a book or off a computer disk, why pay an attorney to do a will or a trust? The problem with this is the "one size fits all" approach does not always work. The pre-printed will or trust might well fit your needs, but then again, it might not. If it doesn't, it might cost your heirs a lot of time and money after your death. When you pay an attorney or other estate planning professional, you are paying for that person's time and expertise. He or she should be able to evaluate your financial situation, and advise you as to the simplest way to structure your estate so that it goes to whom you want, with the least possible hassle, costs, and taxes. However, it is true that there are dishonest and incompetent attorneys. Choose your attorney or other estate planning professional carefully. Talk to your friends and see whom they recommend. Call your local bar association and see whom it recommends. Call several attorneys or other professionals and see what their fees are. Choose one whose reputation and fees you feel comfortable with.

The *PLAN AHEAD* sections contained in this book have emphasized a different, but complementary, sort of planning: making sure that your loved ones know
- your wishes
- all relevant information
- the location of any necessary documents or information

Almost every section of this book has emphasized the need to keep up-to-date information in a place where your loved ones can get to it. Where should you keep such information? Some documents, such as your original will, should probably be kept in a secure place, such as a safe deposit box. On the other hand, some information should be kept so that you have easy access to it, presumably somewhere in your home. What's the best way to keep track of all the documents and information mentioned in this book? There are many possibilities, one of which is noting all the information, including where documents are located, in this book. The following pages are designed to complement the *PLAN AHEAD* sections of this book. Simply note the information here and make sure that your loved ones are aware that you've noted the information in this book and that they know where you keep this book.

Again, this is a complement to true estate planning, not a substitute for it. Noting the information here will help your loved ones after you die. And if you organize this information before consulting with an estate planning attorney, you will save time in implementing your estate plan and you will probably save money.

Immediate Concerns

Are there written instructions with regard to anatomical gifts, funeral, cremation, and burial? If so, where are the instructions located and who has copies? Are the provisions in your will, in a separate written document, in a health care form, in a durable power of attorney for health care, or in other document?

Written Instructions (regarding anatomical gifts, funeral, cremation, and burial)

Do you have written instructions?_____

Where are the instructions located?_____

Who is named to make a decision at your death?_____

Anatomical Gifts

The donation of organs and/or pacemaker needs to be discussed with your doctor or medical service as to the procedure and the organization or person to contact at death.

I wish to donate any needed organs or parts: _____

I wish to donate a pacemaker (If so, date implanted):_____

I wish to donate the following specified organs or parts:_____

Choosing a Funeral Home, Mortuary, or Cremation Society

Funeral home or cremation society to be used at death:

Name:_____

Address:_____

Phone:_____

Preference—burial or cremation?_____

Is there a pre-need contract?_____

If so, location of the written contract and/or cemetery deed:_____

Funeral Arrangements

Do you want some form of service?_____

Location of service—church, synagogue, temple, other?

Name:_____

Address:_____

_____

Phone:_____

Casket at service?_____

Specific hymns?_____

_____

Specific readings?_____

_____

Other specific wishes:_____

_____

Burial or Cremation Arrangements

If burial, do you own burial plot?_____

If so, location of cemetery deed:_____

If not, your preferences on location:_____

If a veteran, do you want a veteran's service?_____

Location of any relevant discharge or other veterans papers:_____

If cremation, disposition of ashes:_____

(Remember that there may be restrictions in your state or wherever the ashes are to be scattered about where ashes can legally be placed. It is important to check on the proposed disposition of ashes).

Finding the Will, Codicil, and/or Living Trust Agreement

Location of original will and any codicils:_____

Date of will and codicils, if any:_____

Location of original trust agreement and amendments:_____

Date of trust agreement and amendments:_____

Location of safe deposit box or boxes:_____

Co-signer on your safe deposit box:_____

Location of safe deposit box key:_____

Executors, Trustees, and Agents

Name and address of agent who has power of attorney:_____

_____

Name and address of agent who has health care power of attorney:

_____

_____

Name and address of anyone nominated as conservator or guardian
for you:_____

_____

Name and address of executor:_____

_____

Name and address of successor trustee of living trust:_____

_____

Obituary

Name of newspaper or newspapers to be used:_____
Relatives and accomplishments to be mentioned:_____

_____

_____

_____

_____

_____

_____

_____

_____

_____

_____

Legal Concerns

Attorney

Do you have an attorney?_____

Attorney's Name:_____

Address:_____

Phone:_____

Accountant

Do you have an accountant, tax preparer, or enrolled agent?_____

Name:_____

Address:_____

Phone:_____

Location of copies of income tax returns:_____

Have you ever filed a gift tax return?_____

Location of copies of gift tax returns:_____

Financial Advisor

Do you have a financial advisor?_____

Name:_____

Address:_____

Phone:_____

Stock Broker

Do you have a stock broker?_____

Name:_____

Address:_____

Phone:_____

Life Insurance Agent

Do you have a life insurance agent?_____

Name:_____

Address:_____

Phone:_____

Casualty Insurance Agent

Do you have a casualty insurance agent?_____

Name:_____

Address:_____

Phone:_____

Listing Assets

1. Real Property

Address:_____

Date purchased:_____

Cost basis:_____

Title to property:_____

Current value:_____

Amount of mortgage:_____

Name of lender:_____

Assessor or county's number for property:_____

Location of copy of the deed:_____

Is there a loan or loans on the property?_____

Location of copy of the mortgage:_____

Name of lender:_____

Address:_____

Phone:_____

Loan account number:_____

Approximate balance due on each loan:_____

Location of last real estate tax bill:_____

Location of insurance policies for property:_____

Name of insurance agent or broker:_____

Address:_____

Phone:_____

*You should list all of these items for each parcel of real property. You should also list mortgage information if there is more than one loan on each property.

2. Bank, Savings and Loan, Credit Union and Thrift Accounts

Name of institution:_____

Branch address:_____

Phone:_____

Type of account:_____

Current balance:_____

Title to account:_____

Passbook certificate or statement:_____

*You should list each of these for each account.

3. Stock Certificates

This section is to be completed if you physically have the stock certificates in your possession such as at home or in your safe deposit box. Stocks held in a dividend reinvestment plan, brokerage account or mutual fund should not be listed here.

Name of stock:_____

Number of shares:_____

Date purchased:_____

Cost basis:_____

Title:_____

Current value:_____

Type of preferred stock (if the stock is preferred):_____

*You will need all of this information for each stock that you own.

4. Dividend Reinvestment Plan

This section is to be completed if you own stock which is in a dividend reinvestment plan, where the dividends buy additional shares of stock. The stock certificates for the additional shares are retained by the agent, much as mutual fund shares generally are.

Name of stock:_____

Number of shares currently in plan:_____

Date originally purchased:_____

Cost basis:_____

Title: _____

Current value:_____

Type of preferred stock (if the stock is preferred):_____

Name and address of dividend agent:_____

Account number:_____

*You will need all of this information for each dividend reinvestment plan that you own.

5. Bonds

The bonds listed here are corporate or tax exempt bonds. Do not list any treasury bonds or United States Savings Bonds.

Location of bonds or statement showing bonds:

Name of bond:_____

Type of bond:_____

Interest rate:_____

Due date:_____

Date purchased:_____

Cost basis:_____

Title:_____

Current value:_____

*You will need all of this information for each bond that you own.

6. United States Treasury Direct Account

Complete this section if you have a United States Treasury direct account whereby you purchase United States Treasury bills, notes and bonds directly from the treasury department or federal reserve bank.

Address of treasury direct account agency:_____

Account number:_____

Location of last statement for account:_____

Name of obligation:_____

Type:_____

Interest rate:_____

Due date:_____

Date purchased:_____

Cost basis:_____

Title:_____
Current value:_____

7. United States Savings Bonds

List all United States savings bonds owned. These include the older "E" and "H" bonds, the "EE" and "HH" bonds, and many recently issued savings bonds. For each bond owned list the following:

Type of bond:_____
Month of issue:_____
Cost basis:_____
Title:_____
Current value:_____

*You will need all of this information for each bond that you own.

8. Mutual Funds

Location of statement for each fund:_____
Exact name of fund:_____
Number of shares:_____
Date purchased:_____
Cost basis:_____
Title:_____
Current value:_____

*You will need all of this information for all of your mutual fund investments.

9. Limited Partnerships

Location of last K-1 Tax Form for partnership:_____
Name of partnership:_____
Are you a general or limited partner?_____
Address of general partner:_____
Date purchased:_____
Cost basis:_____
Title:_____
Current value:_____
Are there restrictions on sale or transfer of interest?_____

If so, how?_____

*You will need all of this information for all of the limited partner-ships in which you have invested.

10. Brokerage Accounts

Name of broker:_____

Name and location of firm:_____

Account number:_____

Title:_____

Current value:_____

* You will need this information for all of your brokerage accounts.

11. Notes and Mortgages Due You

Payor on note:_____

Exact name of payee:_____

Due date:_____

Interest rate:_____

Balance:_____

Title:_____

Security (if any) for Note:_____

Location of original note and other original documents:_____
_____

*You will need this information for all notes and mortgages that may be due or payable to you.

12. Other Assets

For each of the following you need a description of the item, the location of legal papers showing ownership, and details about any loans or mortgages against the asset.

You should also list any insurance such as casualty insurance or liability insurance for each asset.

*This list is not inclusive, so if you own anything else of value, it should be listed.

Automobiles:

_____

_____

_____

Boats:

_____

_____

Airplanes:

_____

_____

Antiques:

_____

_____

_____

Stamp, Coin, or Other Collections:

_____

_____

Copyrights:

_____

_____

Oil, Gas, Timber, or Other Mineral interests:

_____

_____

_____

Business Interests such as a closely held corporation, limited liability corporation, limited liability partnership, or similar interest:

_____

_____

Any other assets of value:

_____

_____

Personal items:

_____

_____

_____

_____

_____

Pets:

_____

_____

If the Decedent was a Trustee, Executor or Fiduciary
Name of trust, estate, guardianship or conservatorship:_____
Name and address of attorney:_____

Name and address of accountant:_____

Name and address of court involved:_____

Location of financial records:_____
Location of legal papers:_____
Name and address of any successor fiduciaries:_____

Casualty Insurance for Assets
For each policy which covers fire, theft, casualty loss or liability coverage, list the following:
Insurance company name:_____
Address:_____
Phone:_____
Assets covered:_____
Policy number:_____
Amount of coverage:_____
Broker's name:_____
Address:_____
Phone:_____

Credit Cards
List for each credit card owned:
Name of credit card company:_____
Account number:_____
Address of company:_____
Phone:_____

Lump Sum Pension, Profit Sharing, IRA and other Benefits

Location of information on plan:_____

Name and address of administrator:_____

_____

Name of person to contact:_____

Account number:_____

Current value:_____

Primary beneficiary:_____

Secondary beneficiary:_____

Other information:_____

* You will need this information for each separate plan that you have.

Life Insurance

Location of insurance policy:_____

Name of insurance company:_____

Address of company:_____

Name and address of agent, if any:_____

_____

Policy number:_____

Face amount of the policy:_____

Current value of policy:_____

Primary beneficiary:_____

Secondary beneficiary:_____

*You will need this information for each separate policy that you own.

Single Premium Deferred Annuity

Location of annuity contract:_____

Name and address of company:_____

_____

Policy number:_____

Name and address of agent, if any:_____

Primary beneficiary:_____

Secondary beneficiary:_____

Current lump-sum value of policy:_____

Cost basis of policy:_____

* You will need this information for each separate policy that you own.

Retirement Benefits

Social security number:_____

Monthly amount of social security received:_____

If direct deposit, location of bank account and account number:

_____

_____

Address and telephone number of local social security office:

_____

_____

Name of other pension plan where benefits are received:

_____

Monthly amount:_____

If direct deposit, location of bank account and number:

_____

Name and address of person to contact:_____

_____

*You will need this information for each separate retirement benefit that you receive.

Employment Benefits

Name and address of employer:_____

_____

Name and phone number of person to contact:_____

_____

Are any benefits payable other than salary?_____

If so, what benefits?_____

NOTES

INFORMATION AVAILABLE ON THE INTERNET

There is a wealth of information available on the internet. Finding what you want is sometimes a problem. Listed below are various sources of general information, available by subject matter. Like many references, some of these internet links may disappear in the future. Some sites also give links to other sites for more information.

To view some of the information you will need Adobe Acrobat reader. This can be downloaded free at (http://www.adobe.com/products/acrobat/readstep2.html).

Anatomical gifts-(http://www.yostandwebb.com/articles/anatomical_gifts.htm). A general reference site with links to other sites is (http://www.ndmed.com/PublicHealth/Anatomicalgifts.htm). Although this is a North Dakota Medical Association site, it gives links to various organ donation organizations.

Funerals-(http://www.funerals.org). Site of the Funeral Consumer Alliance.

Probate laws by state-(http://www.law.cornell.edu/topics/state_statures3.html#probate).

Locating attorneys-(http://www.lawyers.findlaw.com/).
                    -(http://www.martindale.com/xp/Martindale/home.xml).

Social Security-(http://www.ssa.gov/).

Medicare-(http://www.medicare.gov/).

Internal Revenue Service-(http://www.irs.gov/). General site for IRS. Look for the following:
Publication 550-Survivors, Executors, & Administrators
Publication 950-Introduction to Estate & Gift Taxes
Forms and instructions-706 United States Estate Tax Return
                    -709 United States Gift Tax Return

State taxation-(http:www.bankrate.com/brm/itax/state/state_tax_home.asp). This is a mortgage brokerage site with links to all state tax departments.

State government sites-(http://www.statelocalgov.net). Site with reference to all states and subdivision websites.